ELITE SERI[ES]

EDITOR: MARTIN WINDROW

Tank War – Central Front

NATO vs. Warsaw Pact

Text by STEVEN J. ZALOGA

Colour plates by STEVEN J. ZALOGA
& SIMON McCOUAIG

OSPREY PUBLISHING LONDON

Published in 1989 by
Osprey Publishing Ltd
59 Grosvenor Street, London W1X 9DA
© Copyright 1989 Osprey Publishing Ltd

British Library Cataloguing in Publication Data
Zaloga, Steven J.
   Tank war: central front: NATO vs Warsaw Pact.
   Elite series; 26
   1. Military forces Tank units
   I. Title II. Series
   358'.18

ISBN 0-85045-904-4

Filmset in Great Britain
Printed through Bookbuilders Ltd, Hong Kong

Acknowledgements
The author would like to extend his thanks to several
friends who contributed to this book: special thanks to
Pierre Touzin for his fine shots of NATO tank
exercises; to Terry Gander and Christopher Foss for
their kind help in assembling photographs, and to
Mike Hennessy of General Dynamics Land Systems
Division for the IPMI photographs; also to James
Loop, George Balin, Michael Green, Cookie Sewell,
David Isby and Simon Dunstan for their assistance.

Artist's Note
Readers may care to note that the original paintings
from which the colour plates in this book were
prepared are available for private sale. All
reproduction copyright whatsoever is retained by the
publisher. Enquiries about Plates B–K should be
addressed to:
Video Ordnance
P O Box 521
Greenwich
CT 06836
USA
and about Plates A and L to:
Simon McCouaig
4 Yeoman's Close
Stoke Bishop
Bristol
Avon BS9 1DH

Author's Note
By the terms of the Gorbachev peace initiative.
announced since this book went to press, the tank
forces of the Warsaw Pact will be gradually reduced.
The GSFG tank force will eventually lose 2,700 tanks
and, in addition, the Soviets will withdraw one tank
division from Czechoslovakia and Hungary, and one
regiment from Poland. Other WarPac countries plan
to reduce their forces: East Germany by 600 tanks
and Czechoslovakia and Poland by 850 each.

The Battle for Neustadt Junction

By 13:20 on the afternoon of 12 September, 1st Platoon, D Company, 2/66 Armor had occupied its positions to the east of the small German town of Kielbach. The M1A2 tanks were part of a small American armoured task force moved forward to stop an anticipated Soviet lunge for the road junction at Neustadt 15km to their rear.

The terrain in front of their positions was farmland, mostly gently rolling hills. A line of low hills ran perpendicular to their positions about 4km in front of them, giving the Soviets some high ground for their approach. The platoon, commanded by Lt. Timothy Mason, was equipped with four M1A2 Abrams tanks. There were three platoons in D Company: Mason's 1st Platoon was in the centre. The M1A2s were snuggled close to ground in initial hull-down positions; seen from in front, little was visible but the turret roofs and the snouts of their 120mm guns. Mason had received radio messages from the commander of the task force that artillery support could be expected, but would be limited. He had also warned Mason to keep an eye out for retreating Cavalry scouts. At about 13:30, the platoon watched as a tiny reconnaissance drone flew out towards Soviet positions, spotting for a self-propelled artillery battery about ten klicks to the rear.

At around 13:40, a pair of Soviet BRM tracked

A T-80m of the Group of Soviet Forces-Germany with a full array of reactive armour bricks. Reactive armour has a dramatic degrading effect on the performance of infantry anti-tank weapons, but has litle impact on tank-vs.-tank fighting. (US DoD)

scout vehicles approached the American positions incautiously. Mason ordered his unit to hold fire until their identity was confirmed; but the flat appearance of the BRMs could not be mistaken for the higher, boxier shapes of Bradleys. The BRMs were obviously probing for the NATO main line of resistance. Mason allowed the BRMs to approach within 2 km of his tank. He signalled his platoon sergeant, Carl Washington, in the neighbouring M1A2 to handle the left target while his crew took out the right BRM. The M1A2s fired, and two seconds later the Soviet BRMs erupted in a spasm of burning fuel and oily smoke; their thin armour offered no protection against tank guns. Internal propellant fires from their ammunition blew the remaining wreckage apart. As Mason's platoon watched for survivors, they heard the shrill screeching of outgoing artillery. The little drone must have found the approaching Soviet columns.

The lead BRMs had not managed to radio their final positions to their tank regiment 5 km to the rear. Other scout units, probing other areas of the US task force, had been luckier, and managed to radio back their contact point with NATO forces.

An IPM1 Abrams of the US 66th Armor, 2nd Armored Division during autumn exercises in Germany in 1986. The IPM1 differs from the basic M1 Abrams by incorporating the improved armour of the M1A1. (Pierre Touzin)

Maj. Petr Shurkin, the commander of the 178th Guards Independent Tank Regiment, realised that the opposition had been met. Elements of his regiment still in road march were ordered to fan out into attack formations. In all the noise of the road march, Shurkin had not noticed the tiny artillery drone, but as his regiment was in the process of deploying, incoming artillery struck. It was not very alarming at first: the artillery projectiles seemed to airburst harmlessly over his regiment. But in seconds, tiny shapes the size of pine cones began reaching the ground. The unit was rocked by the staccato sound of explosive rain. Small armour-piercing sub-munitions burst all over the regiment, raising a cloud of dust in the parched fields.

Shurkin's unit had been hit by 155mm ICM (Improved Conventional Munitions) projectiles. These artillery shells contain 88 small armour piercing grenades with shaped charge warheads. The grenades can only penetrate a few inches of armour, but the top protection of tanks is very thin. Shurkin halted his command tank to take stock of what had happened. His units were in turmoil. Several tanks were burning, with flaming diesel leaking from their external fuel tanks; other tanks had had blocks of their reactive armour detonated. Tank commanders who had been riding outside the hatches on nearby vehicles had been wounded.

The mainstay of tank units in US Army-Europe will eventually become the M1A1 Abrams. As of 1988, only a single training battalion of M1A1s was present in the US, with all M1A1s being routed to Europe. It will eventually be supplanted by improved versions with depleted uranium armour. (Author)

Other tanks had suffered penetrations of their thin engine decks or roof armour and had damaged engines. Shurkin ordered a temporary halt.

Within moments, his company commanders radioed in their reports. The regiment had started its approach with 93 T-80m tanks, 36 BMP-2 Hedgehog infantry combat vehicles, three BRMs, a battalion of 18 SO-122 Carnation self-propelled guns, and an air defence battery with four SA-13 vehicles and four 2S6 air defence vehicles. The ICM barrage had been very damaging: 18 tanks had suffered enough damage to prevent them moving forward. Most had split tracks, punctured fuel tanks or engines penetrated and damaged; three or four had suffered internal fires and were on the verge of exploding. Most of the tanks could be repaired, but this would take time that Shurkin could ill afford. About 40 tankers were wounded.

The BMP regiment had suffered the most; the BMPs were even more thinly armoured than the tanks, and happened to be in the centre of the exploding artillery barrage. At least 9 BMP-2s had been hit; some were still operable, but had suffered multiple hits in the turret roof or troop compartment. The attack had been far more damaging to the morale of the motor riflemen. The troops inside many of the BMPs had witnessed the horrific deaths of many of their comrades. The dark, cramped troop compartments were garishly illuminated by the fiery flash of sub-munition explosions through their roofs. The blast killed and mutilated any

soldiers unfortunate enough to be under the impact point. This gruesome experience caused several squads to abandon their vehicles in panic. The company commanders had a hard time getting these squads back under control, and many refused to remount their vehicles even at gun point. The BMP-2 platoons moved forward with about half their vehicles, leaving behind a sorry bunch of stragglers. Shurkin ordered the BMP battalion to dole out its remaining vehicles between the three tank battalions. The understrength BMP companies would follow behind the attacking wave of tanks.

The Soviet forces facing Mason's platoon consisted of the 2nd Battalion of 178th GITR commanded by Capt. Vitaly Burlatskiy. It numbered only 22 tanks instead of the usual 31—about two companies in strength. The battalion was equipped with the T-80m tank with reactive armour array. Soviet tank companies are smaller than their American counterparts; their platoons have only three tanks each, compared to four in an American platoon. Still, they outnumbered the American unit about five-to-one by the time they reached the start point. Shurkin decided to give the Americans a taste of their own medicine. His regiment was supported by 18 SO-122 self-

The business office of an M1 Abrams tank: to the left is the 105mm M68A1 gun; the tank commander is to the right, with the tank gunner in front of him. This photo was taken from the loader's station. (Author)

propelled guns. The surviving BRM had found Mason's position, and radioed in its co-ordinates.

Mason's platoon could see the effects of the American artillery strike over the rise, five klicks in front of them. The oily smudges of tank fires curled up, punctuated by the occasional rumble of a tank brewing up. Mason ordered battle stations. The tanks 'buttoned up'; the tank commanders kept their hatches open, but locked above their heads to protect them against the usual Soviet pre-attack artillery bombardment. The Soviets were nothing if not predictable. Sure enough, at around 16:05, artillery started to scream down on their positions. The Soviet artillery was a good deal less effective than the American shelling as the small 122mm projectiles did not carry sub-munitions; they were ordinary HE-Frag rounds. Several tanks had their radio aerials reduced to splinters, or lost their externally mounted machine guns and other

fittings, but at the end of the ten-salvo barrage all the tanks were still intact and running. Artillery using conventional unitary HE ammunition against tanks is not very effective.

By now, the first signs of the approaching attack were evident. You cannot hide tanks, especially fast-moving tanks, which invariably drag a tail of dust behind them, gradually rising 50 or 60 feet in the air before dispersing. Mason called back to the supporting artillery battery asking for additional fire support, preferably RAAMs. The battery commander, Lt. Syd Dworkin, promised a couple of volleys of RAAMs 2,500 metres in front of the platoon emplacements—not enough to stop an attack of this size, but enough to give the Russkis pause. The 155mm RAAM projectile is one of those little-heralded weapons that can make a big difference on the battlefield. Each RAAM projectile contains nine scatterable anti-tank mines. The projectile splits open at a given altitude, scattering the mines on the ground, fully armed. They will rip open the belly of any existing tank.

Capt. Burlatskiy, like many of the Soviet

company commanders, was a professional officer with a tour of duty in Afghanistan behind him. It was an odd posting for a tank commander, with little practical relevance to the task confronting him now. Burlatskiy ordered his unit to assume the usual battle approach. The companies were skimpier than usual, but most had six tanks in line, company commander's tank slightly to the rear, and the BMPs following the wave of tanks about 500 metres behind. Each tank company was assigned a sector of the sky to search for enemy attack helicopters; luckily, none appeared. Burlatskiy noticed some artillery rounds explode in front of his advancing forces, and was relieved that the enemy artillery seemed to have missed their target by a large margin. He had no idea they were RAAM rounds being deposited in front of his unit.

Mason's troops were taken aback when they counted the opposition: they were outnumbered about five-to-one. But they were experienced, and had good positions. Their firing advantages should be able to whittle down the odds. Mason got on the radio and told the other three tanks to hold their fire until 3,000 metres. Some of his gunners were cocky, and boasted about hitting targets further away than

that. Mason was not worried about hitting them; but the T-80m was pretty hard, and even a sabot round could bounce off at longer range. At 3,000m, an APFSDS sabot round ought to kill any tank, or at least give it a good shaking. He was also unwilling to give his positions away prematurely. Only one other tank answered his radio message; he could see that the others had lost their aerials. The Soviets were over 4,000 metres away. He ran over to the two silent tanks and hollered to the tank commanders: 'Engage at 3,000 metres, not before! Hit your smoke grenades when you see me fire mine!' Both other commanders nodded. Sgt. Joe Pinado clambered out of his tank, *D-22*, and replaced one of his shattered radio aerials. Sgt. Jerry Marsh in *D-18*, the tank on the extreme left, took this as a personal challenge and followed suit. Mason was irritated that they should risk their necks in a display of bravado, but decided to ignore it for the moment: his tank commanders were

A T-64B missile-firing tank of a Soviet tank unit in the GSFG. The T-64B fires the AT-8 'Songster' guided missile as well as the normal 125mm gun projectile. The command antenna for the missile is located in a box in front of the commander's station. This version also has an enlarged gunner's sight which may incorporate improved night vision optics.

probably just stressed out and needed some activity to relieve the tension.

First Blood

If the Soviet tankers were any good, they would use the terrain to mask their approach. From the previous week's fighting, Mason did not expect them to do so. The T-80 was very fast and could cover a thousand metres of farm country like this in 60 seconds. He told his gunner to range them every so often. Spec. Tyson kept on the internal intercom with periodic reports: '3,500 metres and closing. . . . 3,100 metres and closing'. The platoon sergeant's tank, *D-21*, was the first to open fire. A T-80 in the centre company was hit at the turret ring. It just sat there. In six seconds, *D-21* hit it with another round. This time it suffered an internal explosion; the ammunition pannier went up, blowing the turret into the air like a carelessly tossed skillet. By now, the other three American tanks were firing. Marsh's *D-18* on the extreme left got two solid burn-outs with his first two rounds. Pinado in *D-22* on the right got two hits, but no evidence of penetration. He kept switching targets, resolving to engage his first hits later. Lt. Mason's *D-20* got a solid hit on the second round, and two more within the next six rounds.

Burlatskiy could see the results of the first wave of firing. Several of his tanks shuddered from solid turret hits. Three came to a dead halt, two burning.

A quartet of T-72M1s of a Soviet tank unit in Czechoslovakia. Soviet tank platoons normally have three tanks, compared to four in the US Army. The matting on the turret roof is something of a mystery; it has been variously described as anti-radiation shielding, or added armour against shaped charges like those in the sub-munitions in ICM artillery rounds. (Sovfoto)

The enemy tanks were a good 3,000 metres away, but were hardly visible; their barrels were so near the ground that when they fired, they hid themselves behind clouds of dust. Burlatskiy was appalled that they could continue to fire accurately through the dust. He ordered his unit to hold fire until the range closed to 2,000 metres—any sooner was a waste of precious ammunition. Each tank carried only about 12 or 15 rounds of APFSDS, and would need every one. Even without orders, his tank companies followed standard operating procedure, turning on smoke generators and firing their smoke grenades. Against an opponent with thermal sights it did more harm than good. The Americans could still see them, but they could not see through the smoke. Burlatskiy hoped that by the time they were through the smoke, they would be within 1,000 metres of the Americans, and would overrun them by sheer numbers.

Burlatskiy had not anticipated the RAAM mines. His tank was one of the first ones hit; the RAAM exploded under the left track. They were timed to go off a second or so after first track contact, so the blast entered the belly of the hull about three feet back. It ruptured the forward diesel fuel tank, and cracked open the ammunition carousel at the bottom of the tank. The 22 rounds of ammunition remaining in the carousel began going off in rapid succession like a string of firecrackers. Unlike NATO tanks, there was no fire containment system, and the automatic fire extinguisher could do little against so massive a conflagration. Burlatskiy was blown clear of the tank through his hatch. The other two men were killed almost instantly as tank No. 200 erupted.

In the 60 seconds from the time of their first shot, Mason's platoon had fired 20 rounds of APFSDS ammunition into the approaching Soviet column. Of these, 17 had struck home. Five had glanced off, or caused only minor damage. The remainder had penetrated solidly and either disabled or destroyed nine of the 22 enemy tanks. Two more T-80s were gutted by mines, and one lost a track to a mine and was immobilised. Ten remained at the 2,000 metre mark.

The Soviet tanks fired blindly through the smoke, with no effect. In the next half-minute, the US platoon registered another three kills. Seven tanks emerged from the smoke at about 1,500 metres. The lead tank got a bead on Pinado's *D-22* and fired. The round took off the armoured box housing the thermal sight, seriously injuring the gunner below: *D-22* was out of action. Mason fired his smoke grenades and was followed by Washington's *D-21*. The spread was enough to cover the US positions. The Soviets got off several more rounds while moving at top speed. Their stabilisation was not good enough to handle engagements at this speed or in this terrain; they scored no hits. One T-80 commander had the presence of mind to order his crew to halt before firing. He got a solid hit on Marsh's *D-18* with a sabot round, which hit the left front of the turret in front of the loader. The round did not penetrate, but the turret was shaken roughly to the left and the race seemed to jam.

The two remaining M1A2s in the centre began firing in rapid succession. Five tanks were hit in the minute it took the Soviet wave to reach the American positions. *D-20* and *D-21* drove out of their hide positions as the remaining two Soviet tanks overran the platoon line. The Soviets were obviously very confused, and could barely see with all the smoke and dust. Both remaining Soviet tanks were gutted by rear shots. *D-20* and *D-21* stood in the midst of the burning debris of several Soviet tanks. Lt. Mason had started to radio back to his stragglers when he saw the steak of a wire-guided missile come whizzing by the tank. The BMP-2s were still about 1,500 metres away and closing. Sgt. Washington ordered his gunner to engage them: the flimsy BMPs blew apart like toys. The BMP

company had already lost two vehicles in the minefield, and had had enough; they began withdrawing. Washington's crew tried to pick them off, but they were able to hide amongst the wrecks.

Mason's tank was beginning to reverse when it was hit in the front by an AT-8 Songster guided anti-tank projectile. Mason had his head partly out of the hatch when it hit; the machine gun mount in front took most of the shrapnel and blast, but he was slammed back into the turret with a sharp gash on the head. The Songster had been fired by one of the tanks that had been disabled by a mine but not destroyed. By this time, *D-18* had its turret back in order. In combination with Washington's *D-21*, they began engaging all Soviet tank wrecks that were not burning or obviously destroyed.

In less than six minutes, the 2nd Battalion, 173rd GITR had been gutted: it had lost all 22 tanks in the attack on Mason's platoon outside Kielbach. Only two BMP-2s survived from the company that had been attached. Crew losses had been exceptionally heavy. The T-80, like most Soviet tanks, has a decided propensity to burn due to the proximity of fuel and ammunition propellant, and the lack of fire compartmentalisation. Of the 66 tankers who started the attack, 52 were dead. Fourteen remained: 12 were severely injured and lay on the battlefield, including Capt. Vitaly Burlatskiy; only two managed to hitch rides with the retreating

An IPM1 Abrams of D Company, 4/8th Cavalry during the 1987 Canadian Army Trophy. The unit insignia adopted for the competition was a version of 'Bill the Cat' from the popular American comic strip, *Bloom County*—see Plate E. (GDLS)

BMP-2s. Mason's platoon had suffered three hits. Two tanks were damaged, but one was immediately repairable. *D-22* would have to be sent back to the rear for repairs. The gunner was severely wounded and the commander badly shaken up. But the Neustadt junction had been held . . . for now, at least. More Soviet attacks could be expected.

* * *

The Bean Count

This fictional account of an engagement between Soviet and American tanks on the German plains in some future conventional war poses a number of interesting questions. What are the critical factors in tank warfare? Are numbers of tanks more important than tank quality? Or can a better trained force with better equipment neutralise the quantitative advantages of a force with mediocre equipment and training?

These questions seem particularly relevant these days. With the Intermediate Nuclear Force Treaty in effect, public attention has begun to turn to discussion of conventional forces in Europe. Talk about conventional arms control in Europe inevitably turns to a discussion of tanks: tanks remain the dominant weapon in conventional land warfare. In an age of missiles and computers, their importance may have diminished since their heyday in the Second World War; but there is still no substitute on the modern battlefield for their firepower, protection and shock value.

A decade ago, there was much talk of 'the death of the tank'. The 1973 Middle East War saw many tank attacks decimated by the new generation of anti-tank missiles. But today, the technological trends have turned full circle. New generations of armour—Chobham armour, reactive armour, depleted uranium armour—raise questions about the viability of many of the tank's enemies. Other anti-tank technologies, like smart munitions, have yet to really prove themselves outside the laboratory. As a result of the decline of anti-tank technology and the vitality of tank technology, the modern main battle tank continues to reign supreme.

Any attempt to limit conventional arms in Europe will inevitably mean dealing with the tanks. The central problem in conventional arms control is the numerical imbalance between the Warsaw Pact and NATO. How great is this disparity? And is this disparity really important in tank fighting? This study will begin by looking at the big picture, the issue of the numerical imbalance, before switching focus to examine how qualitative issues in tank forces, such as crew training and tank design, affect the overall situation.

The imbalance in tanks between the Warsaw Pact and NATO has been the souce of endless debate for the past two decades. It is a complex problem for two main reasons: the lack of precise numbers for Warsaw Pact tank inventory; and the controversy over which tanks should be counted. The United States has the largest inventory of tanks among the NATO countries, but only a fraction are actually in Europe, and it is doubtful whether the bulk of this force could be transported to Europe unless any war was lengthy. The enormous Soviet inventory is quite scattered. A large fraction is in the Far East, and would probably be maintained there even in the event of a war in Europe, in order to keep the border with China protected. How relevant are the Turkish, Greek or Italian tank forces if the conflict was limited to the inter-German frontier and northern Europe? Would France intervene on NATO's side? How relevant are Romania and Bulgaria to any Warsaw Pact efforts? In short, the Warsaw Pact-NATO tank balance can be depicted in many ways depending upon which forces are included and which are excluded.

This discussion will focus primarily on the Central Front: the inter-German border and northern Europe. What would the balance look like in a conventional confrontation between NATO and the Warsaw Pact in this region?

Warsaw Pact Forces

The total tank inventory of the Warsaw Pact is huge, and is usually estimated at about 53,000 Soviet tanks, and about 12,000–15,000 tanks in the non-Soviet Warsaw Pact. However, not all of this force would be involved in a confrontation in Central Europe. To begin with, a substantial fraction of Soviet tanks are very old T-54As and T-55s, serving with low-readiness divisions in the Eurasian heartland. In a prolonged war these might eventually make their way west, but they

would not figure in the initial months of hostilities. The Soviets also maintain a sizeable force on the Chinese frontier. While the equipment facing China is not the most modern, it is substantially better than the tanks used in low-readiness units in the central USSR.

The Warsaw Pact forces present a mixed picture. Analysts generally distinguish between the 'northern tier' countries—East Germany, Czechoslovakia and Poland—and the remaining Soviet allies, Bulgaria, Hungary and Romania. The Northern Tier receive the most up-to-date equipment and are in a geographical position to play a significant rôle in a Central European conflict. The Romanians are an especially dubious ally, and Bulgaria is in no position to act in a war so far from its borders given its modest forces. The central issue concerning the non-Soviet Warsaw Pact (NSWP) forces is their reliability in a war. There have been endless studies of this subject by NATO, without very conclusive results. In spite of obvious tensions between the USSR and its allies, it is worth noting that the Soviets employed a sizeable Polish army in 1943–45, and that these troops fought with some distinction at a time when relations between the USSR and Poland were far worse than they are today. The question is not really whether the NSWP armies will fight, but how well they will fight.

In terms of equipment, the Soviets still maintain three generations of equipment. The first generation, the T-54A and T-55, still constitutes about 38 per cent of the Soviet inventory, and over 85 per cent of the NSWP inventory. These undergo

A T-80 of the Group of Soviet Forces-Germany in 1986, without reactive armour. The fact that the Soviets were obliged to retrofit their current main battle tank with reactive armour is indicative of the marked relative decline in the quality of Soviet tanks compared to NATO tanks over the past decade. (**US DoD**)

periodic upgrading during their major overhauls every ten years. The current programme aims at fitting a portion with laser range finders, improved fire controls, and new 'horseshoe' armour. These tanks are not commonly found in Soviet divisions facing central Europe, but could be encountered by NATO opposite Turkey. The T-62 represents the second generation of Soviet tanks, and makes up about 24 per cent of the Soviet inventory and none of the NSWP forces. It is not really a full generation ahead of the T-55, as it is little more than a stretched T-55 with a bigger gun, and their relationship is similar to the US M48-to-M60 transition.

The first new-generation tank is the T-64; this represents about 18 per cent of the Soviet inventory, and has not been exported. It remained in production until the early 1980s, and is a contemporary of the M60, Leopard 1 and Chieftain, although they differ considerably in firepower. The T-64 would be one of the most commonly encountered tanks in any NATO-Warsaw Pact confrontation. The T-72 is a derivative of the T-64, designed to be cheaper and more maintainable while retaining the firepower improvements of the T-64. It is the first new-generation tank offered to the NSWP forces, and is built in both Poland and Czechoslovakia. It represents about 16 per cent of the Soviet inventory, and about five to ten per cent of the NSWP forces.

When this picture of a T-62M was taken in East Germany in the mid-1970s, the T-62 was still the mainstay of Soviet tank forces. Today, it remains in limited service in the GSFG, but has been largely replaced by the T-64 and T-80. (US Army)

are obliged to maintain very old tanks in their inventory. It would take the Soviets nearly 20 years to replace every tank in service. The formidable task of equipping this large force has generally led the Soviets to cut corners in their tank designs. On paper, Soviet tanks look very good indeed—heavy armour, big guns, good road speed; but on closer inspection, the short cuts become more obvious. The Soviets obviously favour numbers over quality in the tank debate; NATO favours quality over numbers.

The Group of Soviet Forces—Germany

At the heart of any Soviet offensive into western Europe would be the Group of Soviet Forces-Germany (GSFG). The GSFG is the most tank-heavy concentration of forces in the Soviet Army. During peacetime, the GSFG consists of eight motor rifle divisions and 11 tank divisions, formed into five armies. In addition, each of the armies has an independent tank regiment. In total, the GSFG has about 5,700 tanks in its units, plus about 2,000 additional tanks in forward reserves, training regiments and other non-divisional units. At full strength, current Soviet tank divisions each have

The latest Soviet tank to be publicly discussed is the T-80. It is a further iteration of the T-64/T-72 family, and not really a new tank comparable to the M1 Abrams, Leopard 2 or Challenger. T-80 represents less than ten per cent of the Soviet inventory, and is heavily concentrated in units facing NATO. There have been reports of a new-generation tank, comparable to the NATO tanks, but few details are available. Much of the public discussion has focused on US intelligence projections like the ephemeral FST-1 and turretless FST-2.

The Soviet Ground Forces are so large that they

The T-54A and T-55 series remain the most common tank types in the Soviet Ground Forces; however, they are mainly retained inside the Soviet Union in low-readiness units. Many are being retrofitted with laser rangefinders over the gun, like these T-55s. (Sovfoto)

about 330 tanks, while motor rifle divisions have about 220. The GSFG has been undergoing a major equipment upgrade since the mid-1970s. At the moment, the most common tank is the T-64A and T-64B, amounting to about 65 per cent of GSFG inventory. Since 1981 it has begun to be supplemented by the newer T-80, which currently amounts to about 15 per cent of its holdings. The T-62 is the only older type of tank commonly found in the GSFG. It is used mainly by independent tank regiments, training units and the like, and totals about 15 per cent of the current inventory.

Group of Soviet Forces—Germany
(*Tankoviye Voiska*)

2nd Guards Army	*Furstenburg/Havel*
16th Guards Tank Div.	Neustrelitz
21st Motor Rifle Div.	Perleberg
9th Guards Motor Rifle Div.	Schwerin
207th Motor Rifle Div.	Stendal
3rd Shock Army	*Magdeburg*
7th Guards Tank Div.	Dessau-Rosslau
10th Guards Tank Div.	Altengrabow
12th Guards Tank Div.	Neuruppin
47th Guards Tank Div.	Hillersleben/Altmark
20th Guards Army	*Eberswalde*
25th Tank Div.	Vogelsang
32nd Guards Tank Div.	Juterbog
90th Guards Tank Div.	Bernau
35th Motor Rifle Div.	Doberitz
8th Guards Army	*Weimar-Nohra*
79th Guards Tank Div.	Jena
27th Guards Motor Rifle Div.	Halle/Saale
39th Guards Motor Rifle Div.	Ohrdruf
57th Guards Motor Rifle Div.	Naumburg
1st Guards Tank Army	*Dresden*
9th Tank Division	Riesa
11th Guards Tank Div.	Dresden-Klotzsche
20th Guards Motor Rifle Div.	Grimma

The German National People's Army

The German NVA (National Volksarmee) is the element of the Warsaw Pact most closely integrated with the Soviet Army. In the event of war German divisions would probably be integrated directly into Soviet armies and fronts. In terms of equipment modernity, the East German NVA receives the highest priority of all non-Soviet Warsaw Pact (NSWP) forces. The NVA currently fields four motor rifle divisions and two tank divisions. These units are organised along Soviet lines. The T-55 is still the predominant tank type in the NVA,

amounting to about 80 per cent of its 1,800 tanks; the remaining 20 per cent are T-72B and T-72G tanks, mostly of Czechoslovak or Polish manufacture, with this fraction steadily expanding.

German National People's Army
(*Panzertruppen*)

3.NVA Armee	Leipzig
7.Panzerdivision	Dresden
4.MotSchutzendivision	Erfurt
11.MotSchutzendivision	Halle
5.NVA Armee	*Neubrandenburg*
9.Panzerdivision 'Heinz Hoffman'	Eggesin
1.MotSchutzendivision	Potsdam
8.MotSchutzendivision	Schwerin

The Czechoslovak People's Army

The Czechoslovak People's Army (CSLA) is relatively well equipped by Warsaw Pact standards, due to the Czechoslovak industrial base. Since it is one of two Warsaw Pact armies bordering on

Although the T-72 is not widely used in East Germany, it is the most common new main battle tank in divisions in the western Soviet military districts. This particular T-72M2 variant is sometimes called the 'Super Dolly Parton' model due to its prominent armour additions on the turret front. It first began to appear in around 1986, after the basic T-72M1 'Dolly Parton'. (US Army)

The Soviets are gradually upgrading older T-64 tanks like these in the GSFG. This T-64A has had additional armour welded to the glacis plate. The Soviet censor has also brushed out the gunner's sight and other features on the turret.

Germany, the Soviets insist that it maintain a high degree of readiness, and it is generally comparable to the East German NVA in modernity of equipment. However, some of its units do not have a full table of equipment, especially some of the units stationed in Slovakia. The CSLA is the first NSWP force to begin extensive modernisation of its ageing fleet of T-55s. The first stage consists of the addition of the indigenous *Kladivo* (Hammer) fire control system. The second stage includes the addition of Soviet-style 'horseshoe' armour. The CSLA currently fields five motor rifle and five tank divisions. There are about 2,650 tanks, of which about 80 per cent are T-55s, the remainder T-72Bs and T-72Gs. The CSLA supports the Soviet Central Group of Forces (CGF) which currently numbers two tank divisions and three motor rifle divisions. The Soviet tank forces in Czechoslovkia, while not as numerous as CSLA units, are much more modern. There are about 1,550 tanks, of which about 20 per cent are T-62, and the remainder either T-72 or T-64. In the event of war the CSLA would probably be involved in two distinctly different operations. A portion of its more modern forces would be used to support Soviet forces in drives against NATO in Germany. Should the USSR decide to involve Austria in a conventional war, CSLA units would play a prominent rôle in any such invasion along with allied Polish, Soviet and Hungarian units.

The predominant version of the T-72 in service with the Soviet groups of forces in Central Europe is the T-72M1, sometimes called the 'Dolly Parton' model. This was the first version to carry heavier armour on the turret front. These vehicles serve with the Central Group of Forces in Czechoslovakia, and the insignia on the searchlight cover is common to units which participated in the 1981 *Zapad* exercise. (Sovfoto)

Czechoslovak People's Army
(Tankove Vojsko)

1 CSLA Armada	*Pribram*
1 Tankova Divizia	Slany
2 Motostrelecka Divizia	Susice
19 Motostrelecka Divizia	Plzen
20 Motostrelecka Divizia	Karlovy Vary
4 CSLA Armada	*Pisek*
4 Tankova Divizia	Havlickuv Brod
9 Tankova Divizia	Tabor
3 Motostrelecka Divizia	Kromeriz
15 Motostrelecka Divizia	Ceske Budejovice
Eastern Military District	*Trencin*
13 Tankova Divizia	Topolcany
14 Tankova Divizia	Presov

Soviet Central Group of Forces

15 Guards Tank Div.	Milovice
18 Guards Motor Rifle Div.	Mlada Boleslav
48 Motor Rifle Div.	Vysoke Myto
28th Corps	*Olomouc*
31 Tank Div.	Bruntal
30 Guards Motor Rifle Div.	Zvolen

The Polish People's Army (LWP)

The Polish People's Army is the largest of the non-Soviet Warsaw Pact armies. However, Poland's economic difficulties have limited the pace of army modernisation. The Polish LWP would probably have the least vital rôle of any of the Northern Tier forces during a conventional war in Europe. While some of the modernised tank divisions in western Poland might be used to support the Soviet GSFG,

The T-72G is slowly becoming the principal main battle tank of the East German Army (NVA). The NVA acquires its tanks primarily from Poland or Czechoslovakia. This version does not have all the added front turret armour of the more advanced Soviet T-72 variants.

the LWP would probably be used for peripheral operations, notably the invasion of Denmark and Austria. The LWP has five tank divisions and eight motor rifle divisions, as well as a number of independent tank regiments. Its tank inventory is about 3,100 MBTs, of which about 300 are T-72Bs or T-72Gs. In terms of modernity, the Polish Army lags behind both the Czechoslovak and East German armies. The Soviet Northern Group of

Tank attack! A German NVA tank platoon, heavily camouflaged with foliage cuttings, barrels down a forest path during summer exercises.

Forces, based entirely in western Poland, is small, with only two divisions and about 650 tanks; these are evenly divided between T-62s and newer T-72s.

The Polish People's Army
(Bron Pancerna)

Warsaw Military District	*Warsaw*
1 Warszawska Dywizja Zmechanizowana	Legionowo
3 Pomorska Dywizja Zmechanizowana	Lublin
9 Drezdenska Dywizja Zmechanizowana	Rzeszow
Silesian Military District	*Wroclaw*
2 Warszawska Dywizja Zmechanizowana	Nysa
4 Pomorska Dywizja Zmechanizowana	Krosno
5 Saska Dywizja Pancerna	Gubin
10 Sudecka Dywizja Pancerna	Opole
11 Dywizja Pancerna	Zagan
Pomeranian Military District	*Bydgoszcz*
8 Drezdenska Dywizja Zmechanizowana	Koszalin
12 Szczecinska Dywizja Zmechanizowana	Szczecin
15 Dywizja Zmechanizowana	Olsztyn
16 Kaszubska Dywizja Pancerna	Elblag
20 Kaluska Dywizja Pancerna	Szczecinek

The CSLA is gradually upgrading its T-55 tanks with the *Kladivo* fire control system and horsehoe armour. The *Kladivo* includes an over-the-barrel laser range finder, and a wind-sensor mounted at the rear of the turret. (US Army)

Czechoslovakia manufactures the T-72G, like the one seen here on display during a Victory Day parade in Prague on 9 May 1985. The Czechoslovak Army has been slow in receiving these, because some of the production is diverted to foreign clients like East Germany and Iraq.

Soviet Northern Group of Forces

20th Tank Div.	Legnica
6th Motor Rifle Div.	Borne

Other NSWP Tank Forces

The three remaining non-Soviet Warsaw Pact armies have a substantial inventory of tanks, but they are mostly older models. **Hungary** had a total of five motor rifle divisions and a tank division, but in the past year has been reorganising these into brigades. Hungary has about 1,300 tanks, of which

only about 100 are T-72 and the remainder T-54A and T-55. Hungary would probably become involved in a conventional land war should the Soviets decide to invade Austria, in which case Hungarian forces would be teamed with Soviet units of the Southern Group of Forces headquartered in Budapest. The Soviets have the 35th and 102nd Motor Rifle Divisions in Hungary near Kecskemet and Szekesfehervar, and the 2nd and 5th Tank Divisions near Tatabanya and Veszprem. These forces are more numerous and more modern than local forces, numbering about 1,400 tanks of which all but 100 are T-72.

The **Romanian Army** is not well integrated into the Warsaw Pact, and its rôle in any central European conflict is questionable. It has about eight motor rifle divisions and two tank divisions. It has a sizeable tank force of about 1,300 vehicles, but they are all T-54A or Romanian derivatives like the TR-580 (TR-77) and TR-800 of dubious quality. There are no Soviet units in Romania.

The **Bulgarian Army** is one of the most isolated of the Warsaw Pact forces, and has eight motor rifle divisions and five armoured brigades. It has a relatively large tank inventory of 1,900 vehicles, but less than 100 are T-72s. Its rôle in any confrontation with NATO would be directed southward towards Greece or Turkey rather than towards Central Europe. There are no sizeable Soviet combat units in Bulgaria.

Tank Forces in the European USSR

The western military districts of the Soviet Union would serve as the primary reserve for any Soviet

Poland also manufactures the T-72G, which will eventually become the mainstay of the non-Soviet Warsaw Pact countries by the mid-1990s. While it is a perfectly adequate tank by early 1970s standards, it does not compare at all favourably with the new generation of NATO tanks like the M1 or Leopard 2.

Western Military Districts of the USSR

Military Districts	Motor Rifle Divisions	Tank Divisions	Old Tanks*	New Tanks	Total
Byelorussian MD	4	10	700	3,400	4,100
Carpathian	8	4	1,100	2,200	3,300
Baltic	7	3	1,500	1,300	2,800
Strategic Reserve	20	12	5,300	2,950	8,250
Total	*39*	*29*	*8,600*	*9,850*	*18,450*

* Older tanks: T-54A, T-55, T-62; New Tanks: T-64, T-72, T-80

operations in Central Europe. The tank and motor rifle divisions in these areas are at a higher state of readiness than those in any other region of the USSR, and are the best equipped. Divisions earmarked for forward deployment in time of war are sometimes better equipped even than the units in the Group of Forces in Central Europe, receiving newer tank types due to the remoteness of the area from the prying eyes of NATO intelligence. The accompanying table summarises the force structure and tank holdings in this region. The strategic reserve mentioned in the table refers to divisions in the Kiev, Ural, Moscow and Volga military districts.

WP Forces Available for an Invasion of Central Europe

As is evident from the discussion above, the resources available to the Warsaw Pact are formidable; but the entire forces could not be brought to bear during an initial assault on NATO. The Soviets do not make their operational plans public, so precise estimates of the forces that would be employed are lacking. The most authoritative unclassified estimate of Soviet operational plans for a Central European operation was prepared in 1987 by the US Army Soviet Studies Office (SASO). The SASO study concluded that the Soviets would probably form three Fronts, each with two to four armies in the initial wave, with an additional army on each Front available as an immediate reserve. In the initial wave, this would total 15 tank divisions and 17 motor rifle divisions with about 9,000 tanks, and a further four tank divisions and five motor rifle divisions in Front reserve with a further 3,000 tanks, giving a total of about 12,000 tanks in the initial attack. The Soviet invasion force would be backed up by substantial reserves that could be brought forward gradually

The Hungarian Army does not receive high priority in Warsaw Pact modernisation plans; it is still dependent on the T-55, like the company seen here, and has only small numbers of T-72s.

The Polish LWP, once the most modern of the non-Soviet Warsaw Pact armies, has gradually been losing ground in the face of economic problems. Its forces are still equipped with the locally produced T-54A and T-55, with much of Polish T-72 production being exported for hard currency.

The Romanians have embarked on their own production of a T-55 derivative, called the TR-77. Foreign customers for the tank, like Egypt, have been disappointed by its mechanical problems. As is evident here, the main change is in its suspension and engine, which is a complete redesign of the Soviet original.

Warsaw Pact Forces Available in a Central Front War

Forces	Tank Divisions	Motor Rifle Divisions	Old Tanks	New Tanks	Total
Forces in Place					
Soviet Forces—Central Europe:					
GSFG (Germany)	11	8	1,200	6,500	7,700
CGF (Czechoslovakia)	2	3	350	1,200	1,550
NGF (Poland)	1	1	325	325	650
Subtotal	*14*	*12*	*1,875*	*8,025*	*9,900*
Warsaw Pact Forces:					
East German NVA	2	4	1,500	300	1,800
Czechoslovak CSLA	5	5	2,150	500	2,650
Polish LWP	5	8	2,800	300	3,100
Subtotal	*12*	*17*	*6,450*	*1,100*	*7,550*
Total, In Place Forces	**26**	**29**	**8,325**	**9,125**	**17,450**
Adjacent and Reinforcing Forces:					
Soviet SGF (Hungary)	2	2	100	1,300	1,400
Hungarian MH	1*	5*	1,200	100	1,300
Soviet Western Districts	39	29	9,900	11,245	21,145
Subtotal	*42*	*36*	*11,200*	*12,645*	*23,845*
Total Warsaw Pact Forces (M + 30)	**68**	**65**	**19,525**	**21,770**	**41,295**

over the weeks following the initial attack. The accompanying table summarises the major armoured forces available to the Warsaw Pact in a confrontation with NATO. As mentioned earlier, these figures exclude Soviet forces in Central Asia, the Far East and the Leningrad military district. In total, these forces contain 56 per cent of the total Soviet tank inventory of 53,350 tanks (as in early 1988). The initial operations against NATO would involve about 22 per cent of the Soviet tank force.

NATO Tank Forces

Nato presents a much more complicated picture when attempts are made to tally its tank forces. The largest tank force in NATO is that of the US, but only a fraction is directly committed to NATO. Many of the NATO tank forces are outside the Central Front area, including Turkey, Greece, Italy, Portugal, and Spain. A major question is whether France would become immediately involved in a war in Central Europe: the presumption in this book is that it would. Southern NATO forces are excluded from these calculations.

The West German Bundeswehr

The German Bundeswehr constitutes the second largest, and one of the most modern, tank forces of NATO. The Bundeswehr currently fields six Panzer divisions, four Panzer Grenadier divisions, a mechanised Gebirgsjäger division, and a significant number of territorial units supported by tanks. At the heart of the German tank force are 66 regular tank battalions, and 12 tank battalions attached to territorial units. Leopard 1 tanks make up the bulk

of the force; there are 1,845 Leopard 1A1s, 232 Leopard 1A2s, 110 Leopard 1A3s and 250 Leopard 1A4s. These numbers are fluctuating as 1,365 of these 2,437 tanks are being retrofitted with thermal sights which will change their designation. The most modern element of the force are 1,800 Leopard 2 tanks with 150 more on order. These break down into 380 Leopard 2s (modified to 2A2 standards); 750 2A1s, 300 2A3s and 371 Leopard 2A4s. The most antiquated element of the force are 900 M48 Pattons, 650 of which have been upgraded to M48A2GA2 standards, and the remainder of which are kept in storage. The M48A2GA2s are used by ten of the 12 territorial tank battalions. The Germans are planning a new-generation battle tank called Panzerkampfwagen 2000, for use by the end of the century.

West German Bundeswehr
(Kampftruppen)

6.Panzergrenadier Division	Neuminster
I Korps	*Munster*
1.Panzer Division	Hanover
3.Panzer Division	Buxtehude
7.Panzer Division	Unna
11.Panzergrenadier Division	Oldenburg
II Korps	*Ulm*
4.Panzergrenadier Division	Regensburg
10.Panzer Division	Sigmaringen
1.Gebirgsjäger Division	Garmisch
III Korps	*Koblenz*
5.Panzer Division	Diez/Lahn
2.Panzergrenadier Division	Kassel
12.Panzer Division	Vietshochheim

The United States Army

The United States Army has the largest tank force of any NATO army, but only a portion is directly committed to NATO during peacetime. The US Army tank inventory (at the end of 1987) consisted of about 1,703 M48A5 Pattons, 2,535 M60s and M60A1s, 4,810 M60A3s, 2,374 M1 Abrams, 894 IPM1 Abrams, and 3,270 M1A1 Abrams. The US Army (as of 1986) had 54 regular and 45 National Guard/Reserve tank battalions. These consisted of ten National Guard M48A5 battalions; 24 Army and 31 National Guard M60 battalions; and 30

The Leopard 1A1, one of the older versions of the series is still in service in some NATO countries. This particular photo shows a tank of PzBtl 294 in 1974. This unit has subsequently been upgraded with the Leopard 2. (Pierre Touzin)

Another example of the Leopard 1A1A1 tank in Bundeswehr service. The red tape cross and number '34A' are typical NATO exercise markings. The red cross is usually used to designate opposing forces which simulate the Warsaw Pact. (Pierre Touzin)

Army and four National Guards/Reserve M1 battalions. In addition, the US Marine Corps has a further 646 M60A1 tanks. The US currently has plans to acquire a total of 12,000 M1s (of all models) through the 1990s.

The US Army in Europe has about 1,750 tanks in active units, of which all but about 200 (with 8th Infantry Division) are M1 Abrams. In addition, there are 1,400 pre-positioned tanks and about 2,300 in war-reserve stocks. The plans are to have all POMCUS stocks identical to the tanks used in the USA, so units like the 1st Cavalry will draw M1

A Leopard 1A1A1 tank of PzBtl 33. This programme was initiated to bring the turret armour of the original Leopards up to the standards of the later reinforced cast turrets of the Leopard 1A2 and the welded turrets of the Leopard 1A3. The Bundeswehr is currently in the process of modernising 1,300 early model Leopard 1s to Leopard 1A5 standards with the incorporation of laser rangefinders and thermal imaging sights and other improvements. (Pierre Touzin)

The Challenger is currently the newest main battle tank in British Army service. Although its mobility and protection have been widely praised, it has inherited much of its turret fire control layout from the older Chieftain. Disappointing results in recent gunnery competitions have led to a much-publicised discussion about possible replacement or improvement options, with industrial and military interests showing all their long-honed skills in media manipulation. At the time of publication the Vickers company have been given a limited time to come up with an up-graded turret design to match current NATO fire control standards. (Christopher Foss)

Below: A Chieftain tank with 'Stillbrew' armour on service with BAOR in Germany. The Chieftain was the most heavily armed NATO tank of its generation, pioneering the use of the 120mm calibre in NATO. (Terry Gander)

Abrams out of POMCUS. National Guard armoured divisions would draw tanks identical to those used in the continental United States, such as M60A3. This means that about 40 per cent of the US tank inventory is in Europe; and it is estimated that the US would ship a further 2,000 tanks to Europe within a month of the outbreak of war.

US 7th Army—Europe
Major Armoured Units

3rd Bde/2nd Armd. Div.	Garlstedt
V Corps	
3rd Armd. Div.	Frankfurt-am-Main
8th Infantry Div. (Mech.)	Bad Kreuznach
11th Armd. Cavalry Regt.	Fulda
VII Corps	
1st Armd. Div.	Ansbach
3rd Infantry Div. (Mech.)	Wurzburg
3rd Bde/1st Infantry Div.	Goppingen
2nd Armd. Cavalry Regt.	Nuremburg

Great Britain

The British Army of the Rhine (BAOR) is the third largest NATO force on German soil. It is a tank-heavy force, generally having three armoured divisions on the Continent at any one time. Units are rotated periodically, so the listing below is intended to be typical of the formations present in the mid-1980s. The British tank inventory consists of about 880 Chieftains and 325 Challengers. Of these, about 450 Chieftains and 170 Challengers were active in Europe in late 1987. There were also over 100 tanks in war-reserve stocks in Europe. Britain is currently in the process of choosing a new tank to replace older models of the Chieftain. It was originally planned to replace them with additional Challengers; but the mediocre showing of the Challenger at the CAT 87 intramural NATO gunnery match led Britain to consider the M1A1 or Leopard 2. Although the Challenger is similar in mobility and protection to the M1A1 and Leopard 2, its performance at CAT 87 suggests that its fire controls are less well integrated. At the time this book went to press, the improved version, the Challenger 2 with a new turret, seemed more likely than the acquisition of foreign designs.

British Army of the Rhine
Armoured Forces

I British Corps	
1 Armd. Div.	Verden
3 Armd. Div.	Soest
4 Armd. Div.	Herford

The Netherlands

The Dutch Army currently fields four active and two reserve mechanised brigades and two active

The Leopard 2 is representative of the new generation of main battle tanks in NATO. Its seemingly archaic slab sides hide advanced laminate armour that is far more effective than reactive armour in defeating anti-tank rocket attacks. This Leopard 2 belongs to the Dutch 1st Corps, on operations in Germany in the autumn of 1985. (Pierre Touzin)

A Dutch Leopard 2 on exercise in Germany. One of the few distinguishing features of the Dutch Leopard 2s are the Dutch smoke grenade dischargers on the rear sides of the turret. (Pierre Touzin)

and one reserve tank brigades. These units possess a total of 12 tank battalions, five active and seven reserve, which are all committed to the I Netherlands Corps in Germany. Of these units, the active tank battalions are being completely equipped with the new Leopard 2NL (2A1) tank of which 445 were obtained. The reserve tank battalions are equipped for the most part with Leopard 1 or Leopard 1-V (*verbeterd*: improved),

some 468 of which were acquired. The Dutch Army still has 180 Centurion Mk.5/2 tanks in inventory, but these are being sold off to Austria.

I Netherlands Corps

1st Mech. Div.	Schaarsbergen
4th Mech. Div.	Harderwijk
5th Mech. Div.	Apeldoorn

The Belgian Army still employs the Leopard 1 as its principal MBT. There have been a series of modernisation programmes over the years, including the Sabca Cobelda fire control system. The Sabca system was so successful that it was adopted on other Leopards, including those of Australia and Canada. (Pierre Touzin)

The Belgian Army

The Belgian Army fields two divisions, the 1st and 16th Mechanised Divisions, and has six tank battalions. One of these, the 16th Mechanised Division, is stationed in Neheim, FRG, and is subordinate to the I Belgian Corps, headquartered in Junkersdorf. By NATO standards, the Belgian Army is relatively poorly equipped in tanks, being dependent on 334 Leopard 1s ordered in 1967. Although there have been modernisation programmes, these tanks still have shortcomings compared to newer types. There are also about 41 old M47 Patton tanks in inventory, although these are used by reserve units for training.

Canadian Forces Europe

The Canadian Army is the smallest NATO contingent on the Central Front, although a rather visible one in the tank field due to its sponsorship of the intramural Canadian Army Trophy for tank gunnery every second year. The principal Canadian tank unit in Europe is the Royal Canadian Dragoons, equipped with 34 Leopard C1 tanks, which is part of the 4th Canadian Mechanized Brigade Group near Lahr. In wartime, the battalion would be filled out with another squadron, bringing its strength up to 48 tanks. Canada acquired 114 Leopard C1s for its armoured units in the mid-1970s. Aside from a small number used for training in Canada, the bulk of this equipment is pre-positioned in Europe, and would be used to equip units flown in from overseas who train in Canada on the wheeled Cougar AFV. Canada is currently in the process of selecting a new main battle tank, probably the M1A1 Abrams or Leopard 2.

The French Army

The French Army is potentially one of the larger contributors to NATO defence of the Central Front, but its semi-independent posture has meant that its forces are not as well integrated into NATO as other armies. The French Army currently fields 16 medium tank regiments, equipped with various models of the AMX-30 tank; these regiments are about the same size as an American tank battalion. Tanks are also integrated into mechanised infantry and cavalry units. A total of 1,184 AMX-30B tanks were delivered to the French Army by the early

The AMX-30B2 is currently the most advanced tank in French service, while the arrival of the LeClerc in the 1990s is awaited. The AMX-30B2 incorporates the improved COTAc fire control system, a new low light night vision suite and other fire control improvements. The AMX-30B2 is both a new production programme, with some 271 new tanks beginning to enter service in 1982, as well as a retrofit programme. The AMX-30B2 is not up to the standards of other new NATO MBTs like the Challenger, M1A1 or Leopard 2. (Pierre Touzin)

1980s, followed by 271 AMX-30B2s. In the mid-1980s the French Army funded the conversion of AMX-30Bs to the improved AMX-30B2 standard, with about 500 tanks converted by 1988; a total of 693 are planned for conversion by the time the programme is completed in the late 1980s. Three of France's eight armoured divisions are forward-deployed in Germany with the I and II French Corps. French units remain under national command authorities, not supreme NATO command. But in time of war, some degree of NATO operational control over French forces would be likely. Since the mid-1980s, France has been paying greater attention to its rôle in a conventional defence of Europe, and expanding its joint exercises with the Bundeswehr. The French Army currently contemplates acquiring the new LeClerc battle tank in the early 1990s.

Major French Tank Units in Germany

I French Corps	*Metz*
1e Division Blindée	Trier
II French Corps	*Baden-Baden*
3e Division Blindée	Freiburg
5e Division Blindée	Landau

The Danish Jutland Division

The Danish armoured force is the second smallest of the Central Front NATO armies, being only

The AMX-30B remains the most common MBT in French service, until the AMX-30B2 retrofit programme is completed. Although the AMX-30B is fitted with a 105mm gun, this is a different system than the ubiquitous L7/M68 gun so widely used elsewhere in NATO. (Pierre Touzin)

marginally larger than Canada. The main element consists of 120 Leopard 1A3DK tanks acquired in 1976–77. In addition, 106 Centurion tanks were rebuilt in the early 1980s, while 111 remain armed with a 20lb gun. The Danish Army has four mechanised brigades and a reserve brigade. Each of the brigades has a tank battalion, with the reserve brigade using the older Centurions. The three mechanised infantry brigades of the Jutland Division have priority for the better armoured equipment.

The Norwegian Army

The Norwegian Army would not be committed to the Central Front, but is likely to be involved in fighting along the Norwegian–Soviet frontier should war break out. Norway's tank force is small, consisting of 78 Leopard 1s and 48 M48A5 Patton tanks. The Norwegian armoured force includes three tank battalions and three independent tank squadrons which are attached to the one active and six reserve brigades.

Other NATO Armies

Although the other NATO armies dispose of significant armoured forces, it is questionable whether any would play a rôle in the defence of the Central Front. Italy has a substantial armoured force numbering 920 Leopards and 300 M60A1s organised into one armoured and three mechanised divisions with a total of five armoured and eight mechanised brigades. There are no known plans to commit any of this force to the Central Front. Greece has a relatively large, but heterogeneous tank force, consisting of 190 AMX-30s, 106 Leopard 1A3s, 396 M47 Pattons and 950 M48 Pattons. It is highly unlikely that this force would play any rôle in Central Europe, though it might become involved in fighting on the Bulgarian frontier. The Turkish Army presents a similar picture. Turkey has received a total of 2,783 M48 Pattons from the US and Germany over the years,

The Leopard 1A1A1 is a retrofitted version of the Leopard 1A1, with spaced turret armour and a weapon stabilisation system. This particular vehicle was in service with PzBtl 194 during the January 1985 NATO exercises. The frame above the gun mantlet is the protective cover of the PZB 200 low light level night vision system used by the commander and gunner. The sight itself is stowed inside the tank to avoid unnecessary damage. (Pierre Touzin)

of which 174 were upgraded with German co-operation to M48T1 standards. The US has supplied 2,108 upgrade kits to bring most of the remainder up to M48A5 standards. Turkey also received 77 Leopard A1s from Germany as aid, with 150 more programmed. The Turkish Army also received 1,347 M47s from the United States, but they are in poor shape and are being withdrawn from service. In the event of a NATO-Warsaw Pact confrontation, Turkey is likely to be involved along its frontier with the USSR. Any role in the Central Front is out of the question. Spain has 299 locally-built AMX-30E tanks in front-line strength; its 181 M48 Patton tanks are being upgraded mostly to M48A5 standards (162) and M48A3 standards (19). The 375 M47 tanks in inventory are being upgraded locally as M47E1 (330) and M47E2 (45). Portugal has about a dozen M4 Shermans still nominally in inventory, and 68 M47s (41 in storage). Germany provided 66 M48 Pattons which are being upgraded to M48A5 standards.

As is apparent from the tables, the Warsaw Pact has a significant advantage in main battle tanks

The most recent battle tank in US Army service is the M1A1 Abrams. This incorporates the same 120mm gun as the German Leopard 2, but manufactured in the US. The M1A1 has been replaced on the assembly lines by a new variant with depleted uranium armour. This version will be nearly identical in appearance to the current version. (Author)

over NATO. In the event of a conventional war, the Soviet Union would be able to bring to bear about two and a half times as many tanks as NATO at a strategic level. This should not be interpreted to

NATO Armour Forces Available for the Central Front			
	Tank Divisions	Mechanised Divisions	Tanks
Equipment in place			
Bundeswehr	6	4	5,135
US Army—Europe	3*	2*	5,450
BAOR	3	0	850
I Netherlands Corps	0	3	910
Belgian Army	0	2	335
Canadian Forces—Europe	0	1	100
French Corps—Germany	3	0	600
Denmark	0	1	170
Subtotal	*15**	*13**	*13,750*
* Five more divisions with airlifted troops, POMCUS equipment			
Reinforcements (M+30 days)			
US Army			700
France			850
UK			350
Subtotal			*1,900*
Total Tanks Available to NATO Central Front			*15,650*

An M1 Abrams of the 11th Armored Cavalry Regiment during the 1983 'Reforger' exercise. The '74' on a blue square is an exercise marking indicating that this unit was on the side of the 'Blue' forces. (Pierre Touzin)

mean that this numerical advantage would be evenly spread. Soviet operational doctrine calls for the massing of forces to achieve significant local numerical superiority. A 1:2.6 overall advantage could be converted to a 1:6 or even 1:10 advantage by careful operational planning along major avenues of attack. In reading accounts of Soviet tank operations in 1944–45, one is constantly struck by the sheer monotony of German descriptions of Soviet ten-to-one advantages in tanks. The Soviets did not have a ten-to-one advantage in tanks, but were able to skilfully deploy their force so that they did have overwhelming superiority along critical avenues of attack. This is a key feature of Soviet operational doctrine, and one which should not be forgotten when evaluating the numerical balance. The 'bean count' should not be interpreted to mean that each NATO tank will face three Warsaw Pact tanks: some will face a dozen, and some will face none. Soviet numerical superiority enhances their ability to concentrate overwhelming masses of armour at an operational level for a concentrated attack.

Do these Soviet numerical advantages really matter? The fictional scenario which opens this book suggests not. But it would be grossly simplistic to suggest that the balance of conventional power in Europe hinges primarily on tanks. Modern wars are not won or lost simply on the basis of the tank forces; as the fictional scenario suggested, other arms (like artillery) play a vital rôle. Furthermore, there are substantial assymetries in equipment between the Warsaw Pact and NATO in many other key areas such as close-support aircraft, artillery, and logistics. The complex interplay of these forces on the battlefield is outside the scope of this small book. Instead, we will concentrate primarily on the tank issue.

There are ample historical examples of wars in which numerically inferior armies defeated larger armies with more tanks. German tanks killed Soviet tanks at a ratio of about 5:1 throughout 1943. US tanks killed Korean tanks at similar rates. The Israeli Army has consistently out-fought larger tank forces, in some cases better equipped, with odds not dissimilar to those facing NATO. In these cases, quality overcame quantity. There are three principal qualitative factors in tank combat: equipment quality, crew quality and tactics. All three are closely intertwined. For example, tanks are designed around expectations of crew quality. Soviet tanks are designed to be simple to operate, since the designers presume that training will be limited. NATO tanks contain sophisticated features that are only useful if the tank crews are well trained at levels comparable to current NATO standards. Tanks are designed with tactics in mind. NATO tank tactics stress long-range engagements to wear down enemy formations at the longest distance possible. As a result, NATO tanks tend to incorporate more advanced range-finding equipment, better fire controls and other features to make these tactics feasible than do their Soviet counterparts.

Both sides employ a wide variety of tanks, and it would be impossible to cover all the permutations of tank-vs.-tank engagements. The aim here is to examine the more common and more contemporary types that would be seen in any initial fighting on the Central Front. This includes the M1 Abrams, Leopard 2 and Challenger on the NATO side, and the T-64, T-72 and T-80 from the Warsaw Pact. The traditional focus of design has been on firepower, mobility and protection, and we will begin by looking at these features.

An IPM1 of 66th Armor, US 2nd Armored Division during the NATO 'Crossed Swords' exercise in September 1986. The IPM1 has the improved turret armour of the M1A1, but the same 105mm M68A1 gun as the original M1. It is externally distinguishable from the initial M1 by the added rear turret bustle, evident in this view. (Pierre Touzin)

The Qualitative Balance: The Armour Revolution

The past decade has seen the greatest technological revolution in tank armour since the invention of armoured vehicles. Until the 1970s, tank armour consisted of homogenous steel. In recent years it has expanded to include non-steel armours and dynamic protection such as reactive armour. The first breakthrough in tank armour took place in the late 1950s when several countries began to consider the applicability of ceramics to tank protection. The US explored the use of ceramic armour in the T95 programme as a hedge against shaped-charge warheads on missiles. The general conclusion was that the types of ceramic armour available did not offer a significant advantage over conventional steel in most applications. Ceramic armour was not viewed as being suitable for use on multi-faceted surfaces near the vertical plane, such

as turrets, for both manufacturing and protection reasons. While US tests concluded that armour at shallow angles, like hull glacis plates, would be the most advantageous application of a layer of ceramic armour under steel, this was not pursued since existing steel glacis plates were so difficult to penetrate anyway. The Soviets appear to have viewed the matter otherwise. It would appear that the T-64 may have introduced the use of ceramic armour in the glacis plate as early as the late 1960s. However, areas like the turret still remained protected by thick steel belts.

The critical innovation in non-metallic armours came in the late 1960s with the introduction of the British 'Chobham armour'. The composition of Chobham armour still remains tightly classified; it appears to consist of layers of steel and non-steel arrays. This type of armour does not appear to be significantly better than steel in defending the tank against kinetic energy penetrators fired from enemy tank guns, but appears to be able to significantly degrade shaped charge explosive warheads, like those on anti-tank rockets and missiles. Chobham armour was developed as an antidote to the proliferation of anti-tank rockets and missiles on the modern battlefield. It was speeded along by the experiences of the Israeli tank force in the 1973 war, when Egyptian use of Malyutka (AT-3 Sagger) and RPG-7 anti-tank weapons clearly demonstrated the vulnerability of tanks to cheap man-portable weapons. Chobham armour, in various recipes, is incorporated into the current generation of NATO MBTs, namely the M1 Abrams, Challenger and Leopard 2.

Chobham armour exploits the penetration dynamics of shaped charge warheads. Shaped charges penetrate homogenous material better than layers of heterogenous materials. As the blast tongue bores through Chobham armour, it is eroded and diverted as it passes through different densities of materials. Chobham armour has changed the appearance of modern tanks. Until 1970, the goal of tank designers had been to shape the turret and hull front with steep angles to increase the effectiveness of the steel armour and encourage deflection of enemy projectiles. Chobham armour is applied in large slabs more reminiscent of the poorly designed tank layouts of the late 1930s. This seemingly anachronistic look reverses the trend in armour layout from the sleek to the slabby.

In spite of the already impressive armour of the Chieftain, the British Army has begun a programme to add enhanced 'Stillbrew' armour to the turret front for even greater protection. The composition of 'Stillbrew' is still classified, but is probably some form of passive laminate armour. (Terry Gander)

Chobham armour does not make modern tanks invulnerable to infantry anti-tank weapons, but it comes pretty close. To begin with, the weight and bulk of Chobham armour precludes its use all around the tank. As in the case of conventional steel armour layouts, protection varies considerably around the tank. The frontal quadrant, meaning the front, and front sides, is the most heavily armoured. The sides are less protected, usually being armoured sufficiently to withstand heavy calibre autocannon fire. The rear, roof and hull floor are thinly armoured. Chobham armour follows this general pattern, with the main accent being the protection of the turret and hull front. Typical Chobham layouts are about two feet thick, and probably offer protection equivalent to about 600–900mm of conventional steel armour against shaped-charge weapons. This is about three or four times more protection than is enjoyed by the older generation of tanks like the T-64, M-60, Leopard I or Chieftain. Chobham armour does not affect tank vs. tank fighting to any great extent, since it does not appear to have a substantial effect on kinetic energy projectiles, which are the mainstay of tank fighting.

Soviet development of an equivalent of Chobham armour is poorly understood. The T-64 and early-model T-72s are clearly of the 1960s era of armour design. Both have well-protected hulls with an added layer of ceramic armour, but their turrets appear to be conventional homogenous

steel. In the early 1980s the later models of the T-72, like the T-72M, began to appear with thickened turret fronts. This led to the popular NATO nickname 'Dolly Parton T-72', named after the buxom American singer. In the mid-1980s two more versions of the T-72 appeared with even thicker front turret armour, leading to the nickname 'Super Dolly Parton T-72'. It is still unclear what type of armour has been incorporated in these newer types; it seems exceedingly doubtful that it is simply added layers of steel. More likely, it is a type of advanced stratified armour like Chobham armour, but differing in its basic composition. The T-80 probably incorporates this type of turret armour, and the Soviets had another new T-72 derivative, and a slab-sided M1 Abrams look-alike on trials in the 1986–88 period. Nevertheless, Soviet armour development appears to have taken a significant step backwards in the past decade compared to NATO armour. Soviet tanks have traditionally been more heavily armoured than their NATO counterparts; but the new generation of tanks arriving in the late 1970s, like the M1 Abrams, Leopard 2 and Challenger, were faced by the new Soviet T-80 tank which appears to have an interim, and less effective stratified armour.

The main drawback to Chobham armour is that it cannot be easily retrofitted to existing designs. It must be attached in large plates to be effective, and so it does not easily fit the sleek contours of the 1960s' generation of tanks. In the 1970s a German firm revived the notion of using explosive armour to defeat shaped charge warheads. NATO showed little interest in this so-called 'reactive' armour, but Israel jumped at the opportunity. Israel had a large inventory of tanks that could not be retrofitted with Chobham armour due to both a shortage of funds and the limitations of technology. Reactive armour offered a major improvement in protection for less than $100,000, or about a tenth the cost of each tank.

Reactive armour consists of a small packet of plastic explosive contained in a small box, or 'brick'. The explosive is insensitive to kinetic impact, and can only be detonated by the high pressure, high temperature tongue of a shaped-charge warhead. When hit by such a warhead the brick explodes, propelling forward the steel plate at the front of the

A close-up of 'Stillbrew' armour on a Chieftain tank of the BAOR. This appliqué armour probably makes the Chieftain largely invulnerable to frontal hits by shaped-charge anti-tank missiles. NATO has favoured passive armour enhancements over dynamic, reactive armour arrays due to their operating problems. (Terry Gander)

brick. The rapid counter-thrust of the steel plate disrupts the formation of the destructive high pressure tongue of the shaped-charge warhead, rendering it ineffective. The Israelis used reactive armour in the 1982 Lebanon war. The Soviets had probably experimented with the concept before this, as had the US and Britain. But the Israeli use revitalised interest in the concept and proved its combat feasibility. The Soviets acquired captured samples of Israeli 'Blazer' reactive armour, courtesy of the Syrians. In the mid-1980s Soviet tanks began to be fitted with reactive armour arrays, with priority going to tank units in the GSFG. By 1988, this programme had extended to units in the western military districts. Reactive armour has been fitted to T-64, T-72 and T-80 tanks. It has not been seen regularly on older types.

Reactive armour is cheaper than Chobham armour and can be retrofitted to older tanks; however, it is not as effective. The probability of detonation is not assured, and its explosive nature makes it dangerous to nearby troops and crew. Unlike Chobham armour, it does not degrade kinetic penetrators at all, only shaped charges. Its most serious shortcoming is that it is vulnerable to relatively simple counter-measures. By placing a small subsidiary shaped charge at the tip of existing anti-tank missiles, the reactive charge can be prematurely detonated before the ignition of the main missile warhead. Newer versions of existing missiles, like the TOW2A and Milan 2J, can defeat existing reactive armour arrays. Although it has

A T-72M2 'Super Dolly Parton' with attachment points for reactive armour bricks. The T-64, T-72 and T-80s in forward deployed units are being fitted with these attachment points. Older tanks like the T-54, T-55 and T-62 are being retrofitted with horseshoe armour.

been suggested that this can be countered by adding an additional layer of reactive armour bricks, this does not appear to be the case. A double layer of reactive armour would be futile, since the detonation of the initial layer would destroy the layer underneath. The other shortcoming of reactive armour is the collateral damage caused by its detonation. Although the explosion of a single brick will usually not lead to the detonation of neighbouring bricks, it can cause damage behind the brick if the armour is not strong enough. It cannot be mounted on thin (10–20mm) armour as used on tank roofs and rear panels, as the blast will buckle or rupture the area behind the brick. For this reason it is difficult, if not impossible, to fit to light armoured vehicles.

The most important consequence of reactive armour is its effect on small, man-portable anti-tank rockets like the LAW, RPG-7, and similar weapons. These rockets are too small to contain effective tandem warheads, and so will probably remain ineffective against reactive armour for some time to come.

Reactive armour is the best known, but not the only form of add-on armour developed in the 1980s. The Soviets began deploying large, semi-circular slabs of 'horseshoe' armour on their tanks in Afghanistan in the early 1980s. The content of these armour packages is not known, but it probably consists of a steel shell with a non-metallic layer of ceramic armour inside. Horseshoe armour has been fitted to Soviet T-55 and T-62 tanks; it began to

appear on Czechoslovak T-55 tanks in 1988, and is likely to begin appearing on East German and Polish tanks in the near future. Add-on slabs of armour have also appeared on the hull front of Soviet T-64 and East German T-72G tanks, but its composition is unknown. The British Army has a similar programme, called 'Stillbrew', to retrofit its Chieftain tanks in the BAOR. The composition of Stillbrew armour is still tightly classified, but it appears to be a passive appliqué armour, rather than a reactive armour array.

The most advanced form of tank armour now in existence is the American depleted uranium armour (DUA), first disclosed in 1988. DUA is an evolutionary outgrowth of Chobham armour, and incorporates depleted uranium in a mesh inside a layer of steel within the armour array. According to the limited public information on the subject, it is capable of defeating all known and foreseen anti-armour projectiles. As in the case of all forms of heavy armour, it will probably be limited in use to the frontal quadrant of the improved M1A1 Abrams (referred to here in the fictional scenario as M1A2), not around the whole vehicle. US sources claim that it will take the Soviets a decade to develop a comparable armour system.

Tank protection is not limited to exterior armour; it also extends to limiting the damage caused when a tank is hit. Israeli experience has shown that tanks can be knocked out five or six times, yet still be repairable and fight again. Modern tank battles are enormously destructive. In their short war in Lebanon, against opponents with very modest armour, the Israelis had 300 tanks knocked out, about 30 per cent of the attacking force. Recovery of damaged tanks, and damage limitation, is essential to prevent total exhaustion of the supply of tanks on the modern battlefield. Of the 300 Israeli tanks knocked out in 1982, 108 were severely damaged, including 92 with penetrations. Of these 92, 52 were destroyed by internal fires that followed the penetration. In other words, while the attacking forces lost nearly 300 tanks in the fighting, about 65 per cent suffered only modest damage that could be readily repaired, while only 17 per cent were totally destroyed.

The critical feature of damage limitation is to prevent the ignition of fuel and ammunition which can lead to catastrophic internal explosions and

1: Corporal, British 1st Royal
   Tank Regiment, BAOR
1A: British tank crewman, NBC gear
2: Stabsfeldwebel, Bundeswehr
   Panzertruppen, summer
3: Oberfeldwebel, Bundeswehr
   Panzertruppen, winter

1A

1

2

3

A

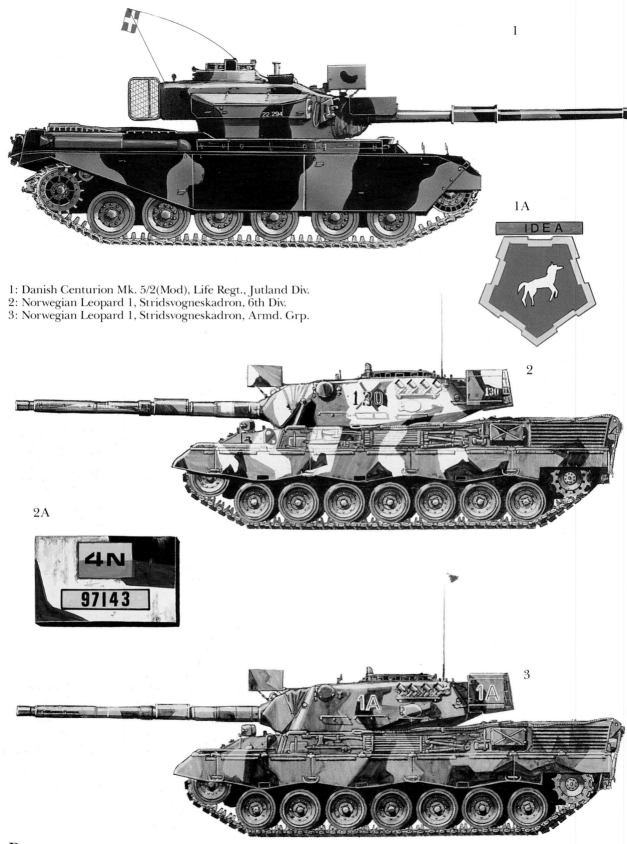

1

1A

IDEA

2

2A

4N

97143

3

1: Danish Centurion Mk. 5/2(Mod), Life Regt., Jutland Div.
2: Norwegian Leopard 1, Stridsvogneskadron, 6th Div.
3: Norwegian Leopard 1, Stridsvogneskadron, Armd. Grp.

B

3B ЗИП ТОПЛИВО

1: Soviet T-55A(M), Ukrainian Military District
2: Czechoslovak T-55A(M)-Kladivo, 1988
3: Soviet T-64B, Central Grp. of Forces; Czechoslovakia, 1988

2A

3 A 190/2

C

M1A1 Abrams, 64th Armor, US 3rd Inf. Div., FRG
1: Tank 1, 2nd Plt., C Co., 1st Bn.
2: Tank 3, 3rd Plt., D Co., 3rd Bn.
3: Tank 4, 1st Plt., A Co., 2nd Bn.
4: Tank 3, 3rd Plt., B Co., 4th Bn.

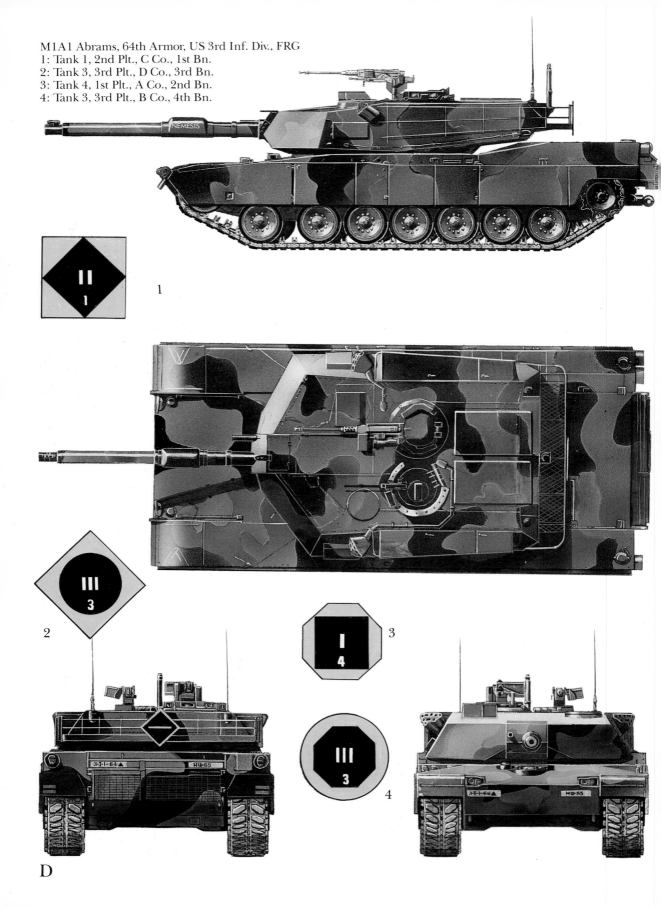

1

2

3

4

D

1: IPM1 Abrams, D Co., 4/8th Cav., US 3rd Armd. Div.; CAT-87
1A, 1B, 1C: Right & left, and rear, turret markings

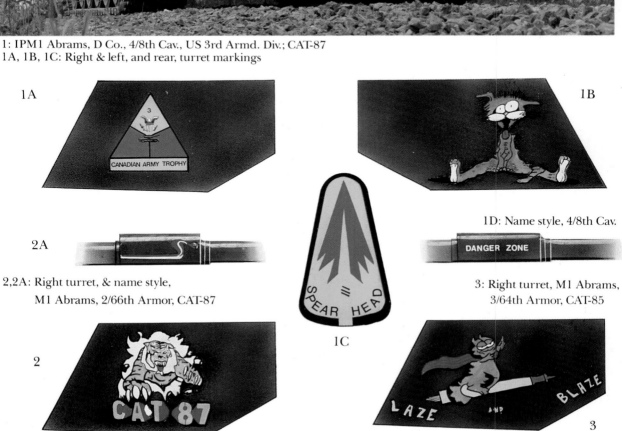

1A

CANADIAN ARMY TROPHY

1B

1D: Name style, 4/8th Cav.

2A

DANGER ZONE

2,2A: Right turret, & name style,
     M1 Abrams, 2/66th Armor, CAT-87

SPEAR HEAD

3: Right turret, M1 Abrams,
   3/64th Armor, CAT-85

1C

2

CAT 87

LAZE AND BLAZE

3

E

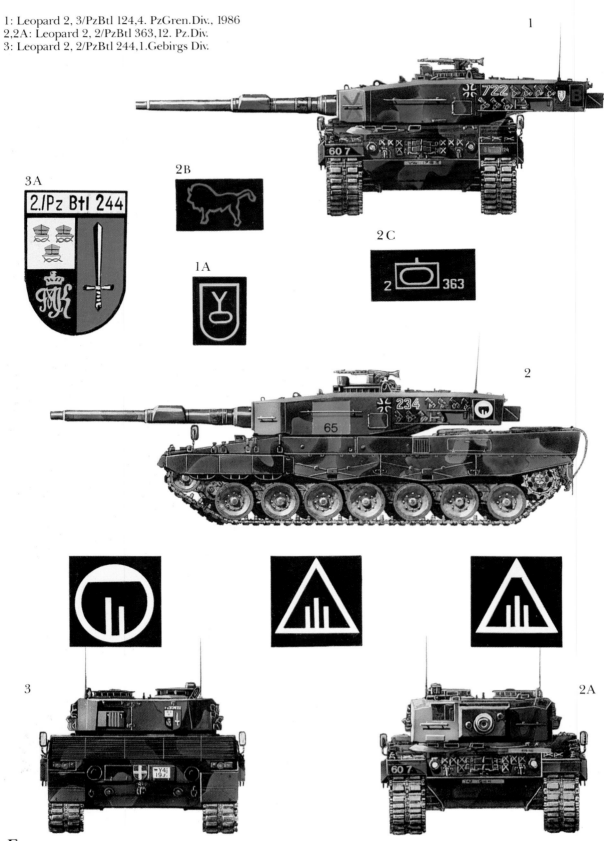

1: Leopard 2, 3/PzBtl 124,4. PzGren.Div., 1986
2,2A: Leopard 2, 2/PzBtl 363,12. Pz.Div.
3: Leopard 2, 2/PzBtl 244,1.Gebirgs Div.

3A

2.lPz Btl 244

2B

2C

2 | 363

1A

1

2

3

2A

F

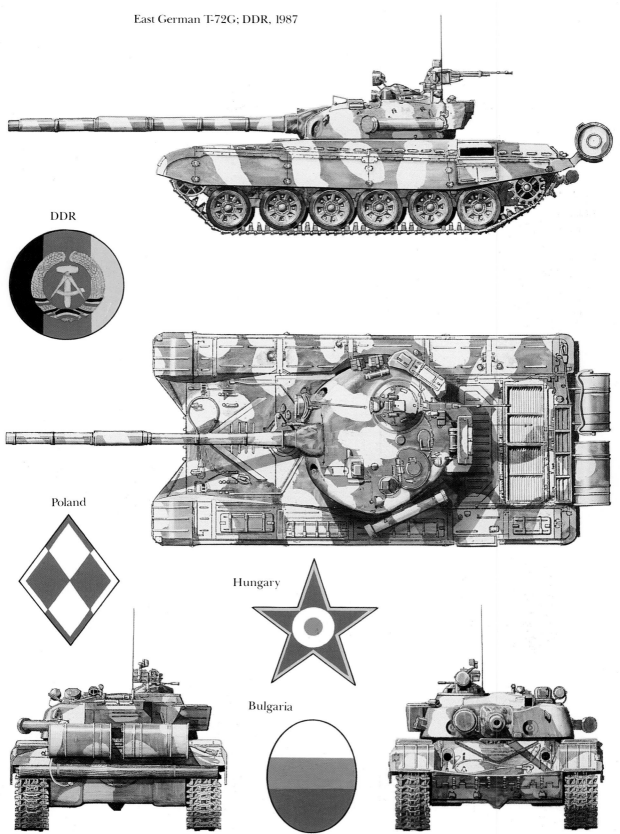

East German T-72G; DDR, 1987

DDR

Poland

Hungary

Bulgaria

G

1: Dutch Leopard 2A1, 43^e Tankbataljon, 41^e Panserbrigade, 1 Korps; CAT-85
2: Greek Leopard 1A3, 1986
3: Canadian Leopard C1, Royal Canadian Dragoons, CAT-87

1

CAT '85

AGOETI

1A

1B

2

2A

3A

3

3B

H

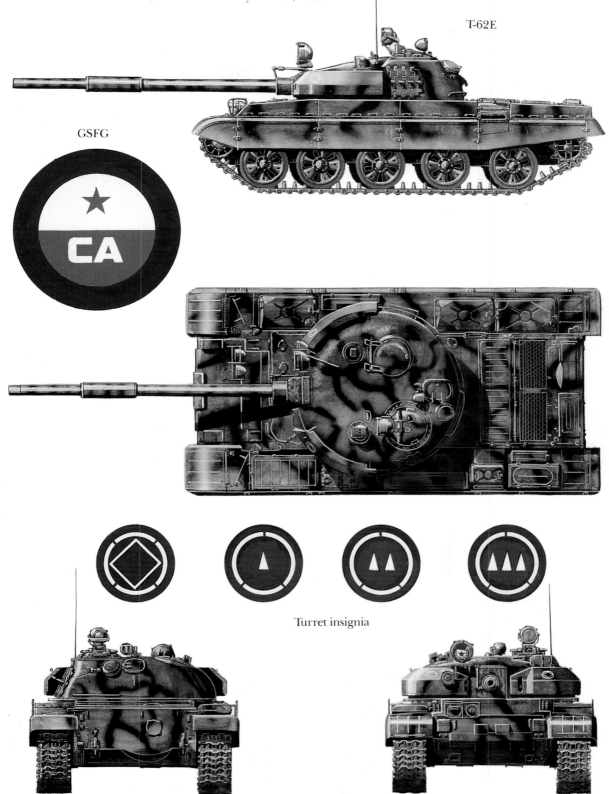

T-62E, Berlin Separate Tank Regt., Soviet 6th Gds.
Mot. Rifle Div.; Turkestan Military District, 1986

T-62E

GSFG

Turret insignia

I

1,1A; Chieftain, Armd. Sqn., Berlin Bde., BAOR
2,2A: Challenger, The Royal Hussars, 1 Armd. Div., BAOR

1

2B

2

2C

2D

1A

2A

J

T-80, Group of Soviet Forces – Germany; DDR, 1988

Guards insignia

A   B   C   D

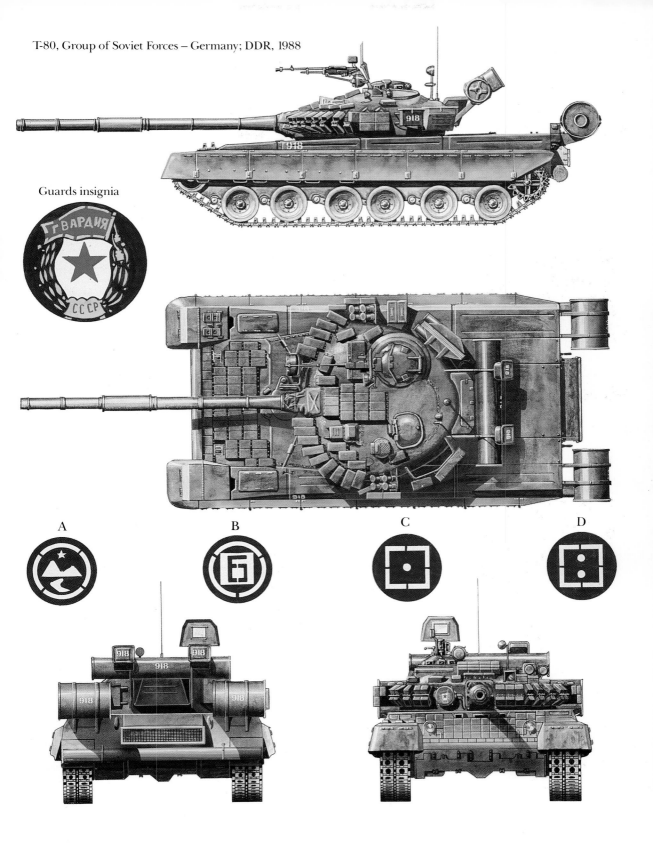

K

1: Czechoslovak corporal tank crewman
2: East Germany tank crew lieutenant
3: Soviet Ground Forces Observer, 1988

L

fires which will permanently destroy the tank. Damage limitation can be designed into a tank by the incorporation of automatic fire suppression systems and careful placement of ammunition. Most new generation NATO tanks have an automatic HALON fire suppression system which quickly overwhelms fuel and hydraulic fires. Soviet tanks do not appear to be as well protected. Tank design philosophy regarding ammunition placement varies. British practice is to use split ammunition, with the very dangerous propellant cases placed below the turret ring. US and German philosophy holds that split ammunition degrades rate of fire, and so relies on blast venting systems to reduce the impact of ammunition fires. Ammunition on the M1 Abrams and Leopard 2 is mainly contained in the turret rear, behind special blast doors. In the event of a propellant fire, the doors prevent the fire from spreading into the rest of the tank, and any propellant explosion is ducted upwards through special blast panels in the roof, keeping it away from the crew. Soviet philosophy relies on keeping the ammunition low in the hull; however, once a propellant fire begins, there are no barriers. Israeli tankers in 1982 found that the T-72 burned just as readily as the earlier T-62. Soviet tanks are particularly susceptible to devastating internal fires due to the proximity of so much flammable and explosive material in so small an interior.

Generally speaking, current NATO tank design has decided advantages in protection over Warsaw Pact tanks. NATO front-line tank types offer distinctly superior armour protection. New technologies like DUA ensure a NATO edge in this area. Furthermore, NATO designs like the M1A1 Abrams and Leopard 2 have features which limit the amount of damage caused by a penetration of the armour, and hold out the hope that a damaged vehicle will live to fight another day, as will its crew.

These advantages extend to tank recovery as well. As is evident from the Israeli experience mentioned above, tank recovery is vital since many knocked-out vehicles can be returned to service relatively quickly. In prolonged conflicts, it is not unusual for tanks to be put out of action on average five or six times during the course of the war, either by enemy action or serious mechanical breakdown. It is imperative to recover these vehicles and return them to service. NATO armies tend to have a larger number of armoured recovery vehicles (ARV) than their Warsaw Pact counterparts: Soviet units tend to have about one ARV per 14 tanks; in the Bundeswehr, the ratio is double, 1:7, and in the US Army, 1:6. Furthermore, the NATO vehicles tend to be larger and more capable than their Soviet counterparts. Vehicles like the American M88 and German Bergepanzer have heavy lift cranes and greater towing power than their Soviet counterparts like the BTS-2, and are capable of more elaborate maintenance work.

Tank Firepower

A tank's offensive power rests in its gun and fire control system. As in the case of armour protection, there have been revolutionary changes in the past decade. The most important have not occurred in the actual power of the main guns, though these too have continued to increase. Instead, the changes have come in fire control, gun stabilisation and crew training.

Current tank designs on both sides of the inter-German border rely on guns in the 120–125mm size range. These guns pack enormous power when firing kinetic energy penetrators. In terms of penetration, these weapons can cut through virtually any known tank armour with the possible exception of the new generation of DU armour. Two types of kinetic energy penetrators pre-

The reactive armour on the T-64A is similar, but not identical, in layout to that on a T-80. This is a T-64A with a Soviet tank regiment in the Central Group of Forces, Czechoslovakia. (US Army)

dominate: tungsten carbide and depleted uranium. The US Army favours depleted uranium, since it has pyrophoric qualities on impact with the steel armour of an opponent: it showers the interior of a tank with a supersonic spray of incandescent metal fragments which shatter man and machine and ignite any fuel or propellant spilled by their impact. The main drawback to its wider adoption is the extreme difficulty of manufacturing and machining this extremely poisonous metal. The Soviets have tended to favour tungsten carbide for advanced penetrators.

Although NATO and Warsaw Pact guns are quite similar in penetration capability, they vary in terms of barrel life and projectile dispersion. NATO tank gun tubes are manufactured to ensure adequate performance through 400 rounds. Soviet gun tubes have not proven to be as durable, lasting about 120 rounds before severe erosion sets in. The Soviets feel that tanks in combat have a short life expectancy and any additional metallurgical improvements will be excessively costly. However, this parsimony forces the Soviets to limit peacetime gun firing, and would lead to a quicker decrease in gun accuracy during wartime. Soviet tank ammunition tends to suffer from greater dispersion at range than NATO ammunition due to poorer propellant technology. The 2A46 125mm Rapira 3 gun is an enormously destructive gun, but it has a mediocre reputation for accuracy at ranges over 1,500m, more due to ammunition shortcomings than to any inherent design flaw in the gun.

A heavy layer of explosive armour bricks on a T-64A in Czechoslovakia. These bricks are very effective in preventing the penetration of the main armour by shaped charge anti-tank weapons, like infantry AT rocket launchers. (US Army)

The real revolution in firepower has come in the area of fire controls. Since the first crude gun stabilisers on American M4 Sherman tanks in the Second World War, tank designers have sought to develop ways to permit tanks to fire accurately on the move. Generations of tanks since 1945 have made incremental steps towards this goal with one-axis stabilisation, two-axis stabilisation, and finally full three-axis stabilisation. Tanks like the Leopard 2, M1 and Challenger can accurately engage moving enemy tanks at ranges of 2,000m while moving at high cross-country speeds themselves, and still have a high expectation of a first round hit. Firing on the move is an important feature for a tank, since it makes it much more difficult for enemy weapons to be brought to bear. An evading tank is much more difficult to hit than a stationary one. In a modern tank fire control system, the gunner places the reticle on the opposing tank, and locks it on; the tank's computer and inertial sensors adjust the barrel in elevation and traverse to compensate for vehicle movement thereafter.

The Soviets have been unwilling to invest in three-axis stabilisation, settling for simpler two-axis stabilisation. This allows fire from a slowly moving tank (12km/h) against a stationary or slow-moving opponent, but with a lower probability of hit than in the case of a full stabilisation system.

Tank gun accuracy is affected by a wide variety of environmental factors including cross-wind, temperature, barrel wear, barrel warp and propellant temperature. Modern microchip technology has finally made it possible for tank fire controls to compensate for these factors. Current NATO tanks use small ballistic computers which accept data from several sensors to determine these factors. Tanks now sprout wind sensors over their turret, muzzle reference systems to determine barrel warp at their tip, and thermal sleeves to reduce the amount of barrel warp. One of the most critical bits of data in a tank engagement is range to target, in order to compensate for the drop in shot due to gravity. The current generation of tanks use laser rangefinders for this purpose, which has greatly increased tank gun accuracy.

In general, Soviet tank fire control technology has lagged behind NATO standards. The Soviets have kept pace in rangefinders, fielding lasers on their current generation of tanks, and retrofitting laser rangefinders to older T-55 and T-62 tanks. But Soviet microchip technology has not kept pace with NATO, and Soviet ballistic computers tend to be a generation behind. As a result, the Soviets have not yet introduced barrel warp reference systems, wind sensors, automatic temperature or ammunition inputs. It is difficult to determine precisely how much this would affect tank combat, since these NATO fire control enhancements probably add only a few percentage points to kill probability.

Another critical innovation in tank fire controls has been in the area of night vision. Night fire controls have gone through three generations. The first generation, active infrared illumination, was pioneered by the Germans in the Second World War. This became the basis of all early post-war Soviet and NATO night fighting systems. The problem with this method is that the infrared searchlights are very obvious to opposing tanks also fitted with infrared viewers. In the early 1970s the United States pioneered the first generation of passive night vision equipment, using image intensification technology. These sights pick up the small amounts of ambient moonlight and starlight and amplify them to create an image. The main drawback to this technology is that it is ineffective on heavily overcast nights or when there is little ambient light. Nevertheless, this was a major advance in night fighting capability, and still remains a principal form of night fire control technology for many NATO and Warsaw Pact tanks.

The third generation of night fighting technology was pioneered by the United States in the late 1970s, and is called thermal imaging or FLIR (forward looking infrared). FLIR technology is by far the most effective form of night vision fire control. Unlike image intensification, it is dependent on radiant infrared energy from the target rather than on natural illumination. A thermal imager detects the minute temperature differences between a tank and the natural background. Tanks are easily detectable. If the engine is running, they give off considerable infrared energy. Even if the engine is not running, tanks tend to absorb considerable amounts of heat during the daytime from the sun, and this energy is gradually dissipated in the cooler night environment. The main drawback to thermal imaging sights is their high

A T-72M2 'Super Dolly Parton' with a full set of attachment points for reactive armour, in the Carpathian Military District.

cost. They typically cost about $100,000 ore more, often amounting to a tenth of the total cost of the tank.

In many respects, thermal imaging technology is as important an advance in tank combat as radar technology was in jet fighter combat. Thermal imagers enable tanks to fight day and night. Not only are they useful in night fighting, but they also make target detection much easier in daylight. The modern battlefield is invariably shrouded in smoke and dust, and normal optical sights are often blinded. Thermal sights can see through smoke and most atmospheric obscurants. Even when there is no smog over the battlefield, they are invaluable in target detection.

Take the example of a NATO tank unit moving forward towards a Warsaw Pact tank ambush. The Warsaw Pact T-72 tanks are hidden and well camouflaged. To a tank with normal day sights, the T-72s are difficult, if not impossible, to detect. To a tank with a thermal imager, the natural terrain is a monotonous and uniform mass, punctuated by the bright glow of several tanks giving off characteristic infrared emissions from their sun-baked glacis plate and their engine exhausts. The NATO tanks can turn the tables on such an ambush. As few Warsaw Pact tanks have thermal imagers, the NATO tanks pop their smoke grenades, obscuring their position. They move forward into the smoke in an evasive pattern so that the Warsaw Pact tanks can no longer see them. The NATO tanks keep the

Warsaw Pact tanks in their sights using the thermal imager, and dispatch them in rapid succession while firing on the move. The ambushers become the ambushed. The advantages of thermal sights were also depicted in the fictional scenario at the beginning of this book.

Advances in fire control technology constitute the most important advance in tank combat over the past decade. Tank fire control improvements make it possible to fight equally well by day and night, and extend the range of effective tank fighting from about 1,000m to well over 2,000m. A moving M1 tank can hit a moving opponent at night at twice the range of a stationary M60A1 tank against a stationary target with about the same probability of kill.

This is the one area where Warsaw Pact tank technology has fallen furthest behind. Soviet electronics technology is simply not as good as electronics developed in the West in terms or durability of performance. The Soviets suffer from a generational lag in mass production of many advanced electronics components, and the components they do produce tend to go to higher

priority platforms such as aircraft and attack helicopters. The Soviets have not yet fielded thermal imaging night sights on tanks as far as is known and still rely on image intensification as their primary passive night fighting sight. The Soviets have tended to rationalise these shortcomings in their military press on a number of grounds. To begin with, fire control advances affect long range engagements (over 1,000m). At close ranges, like 500–750m, an elementary gunner's sight like that on the T-55 has as much probability of accurately engaging a target as the sophisticated fire control suite in the Leopard 2. A German study found that over half the terrain on the inter-German border has sighting ranges of 500m or less, and that only ten per cent has sighting ranges of over 2,000m. The Soviets have argued that the incremental improvement offered by current fire controls cannot justify their increase in cost and complexity. From continuous Soviet attempts to improve their tanks in this regard, these arguments appear to be excuses to hide technological inferiority rather than serious arguments in favour of simple fire controls.

Indeed, one of the most peculiar changes in Soviet tank firepower has been their sudden interest in gun-fired guided missiles like the AT-8 Songster. This missile is radio-guided, and somewhat resembles the Shillelagh missile fitted to American tanks like the M60A2 and M551 Sheridan in the 1970s. This type of weapon has been abandoned in

The Soviet Ground Forces have been retrofitting older tanks like the T-54A, T-55 and T-62 with panels of 'horseshoe' armour as on this T-62 of the Berlin Tank Regiment returning to the USSR from Afghanistan. The exact composition of this armour is uncertain, but probably contains non-metallic armour laminates inside the turret and glacis appliqués. This tank also has a laser-rangefinder over the main gun tube. (US DoD)

NATO as modern fire control offers superior accuracy without the cost and complexity associated with the missile itself. The Soviets appear to have been forced to adopt this weapon for long-range engagements to cover the gap they face in long-range tank battles due to their inferiority in fire controls. The problem is that the AT-8 Songster relies on a shaped-charge warhead, at a time when shaped-charge warheads are nearly totally ineffective against the frontal armour of modern NATO tanks. The M1 Abrams has been tested against shaped charge warheads over 135mm calibre and avoided penetration of the turret and hull. The Songster is below this in calibre and penetration, and newer US tanks like the M1A1 with DU armour are even harder targets.

Crew Training

The one area most affected by crew training is tank gunnery; training cannot have much effect on either mobility or protection, but good crew training can considerably enhance or degrade the effectiveness of modern fire control systems. This is another area where NATO has significant advantages. NATO crew training tends to be far more extensive and demanding than typical Warsaw Pact training. NATO crews are expected to engage enemy tanks much quicker, and with a higher degree of accuracy, than typical Soviet crews.

Just how important a factor is tank gunnery in battle? There have been several attempts to quantify this by operational research. Extensive Israeli–American operational research after the 1973 Middle East War supported the view that target acquisition and rapid engagement were vital in tank fighting, but details are lacking due to remaining security restrictions on these studies. One of the few unclassified operational studies of tank fighting now available was conducted after the Korean War, and examined engagements between US and North Korean tanks in 1950. M4 and M26 tanks which engaged the North Korean tanks first had an exchange rate 16 to 33, meaning 16 to 33 enemy tanks knocked out for every US tank lost. In contrast, tanks which fired after having been engaged first by enemy tanks had an effectiveness ratio of only 0.5 to 1.3. The study concluded that the ability to engage the enemy first was the single most important tactical factor in tank fighting of all factors examined, and the most important factor in raising the effectiveness of tanks in combat. The

The US Army developed its own reactive armour package for the M60A3 tank. Officially called 'Appliqué Armor', it used M1 and M2 explosive tiles to cover the turret and hull. The programme was eventually mothballed due both to the assumption that US units in Europe would eventually be equipped only with the M1 Abrams, and to concerns over the shortcomings of reactive armour. (US Army APG)

A German tanker of the Armour School in front of a Leopard 2 displaying the tools of the trade. To the left is a HEAT training round, and to the right a cutaway training model of the APFSDS anti-tank round. HEAT shaped-charge rounds have largely fallen out of favour with NATO as anti-tank rounds, owing to the development of improved APFSDS rounds, and the Soviet use of reactive and other forms of improved armours. (Michael Green)

ability to acquire and fire on an enemy tank first is dependent both on equipment—such as precise, easy-to-use sights—and good crew training.

Soviet tank training is hindered by the lack of durability of Soviet tanks. Soviet tanks have shorter barrel and engine life than comparable NATO tanks. As a result, Soviet tank units are more restricted in training time than NATO tank units. For example, US tank crews will fire 100–200 rounds of live tank ammunition during annual training. Although some prime Soviet divisions may fire over 50 rounds per crew, 20 rounds per crew seems more common. Much of Soviet gunnery training is accomplished with a 23mm sub-calibre device. While this may be useful in teaching aiming to the gunner, it is not very useful in fostering crew interaction and proper gun drill. It avoids the cycle of loading the weapon, the turmoil of gun firing and the problems of clearing the casing and reloading the gun. The whole cycle of gun firing is reduced to an unrealistically easy drill. The lack of engine

durability on Soviet tanks limits the number of occasions under which whole units are trained; Soviet tank training is usually limited to company-sized activity. It seldom permits large-scale battalion exercises beyond simple road marches, since at any one time only a company or so of tanks is used for training purposes, with the rest being conserved.

The lack of available time and ammunition to train tends to lead to a less demanding standard of gunnery training. The training is further degraded by the usual 'peacetime rot' induced by officer career considerations. Unit training is the responsibility of the unit political officer. The political officer will not enjoy career advancement unless his unit scores well on tank gunnery trials; nor will the tankers enjoy leave or other benefits if their scores are low. As a result, scoring is generous, and demands on the crew are lax compared to NATO practices.

Under the typical training routine, Soviet tankers are expected to engage and destroy an enemy tank at their maximum effective range in 60 seconds. This consists of the following norms. The tank commander is expected to discover and designate the target in ten seconds. He then instructs his crew what type of ammunition to load, and the gunner makes final adjustments on the target based on other inputs such as the laser rangefinder. The crew is allotted a further 20 seconds to get off the first round. Since the effective range is defined as the range at which the tank has a 50 per cent probability of kill, two more rounds are required to bring the kill probability up to over 80 per cent. The effective range of the 100mm gun on the T-55 is 1,500m, so the target is engaged at this range. The crew is alloted 15 seconds each for the second and third round, bringing the total engagement time up to 60 seconds. Crews are scored from one to five, five being 'outstanding', four being 'good' and three being satisfactory; scores of three to five are considered acceptable. But the training cycle is so generous that it is expected that six out of seven (86 per cent) of the crews will pass with grades of four or five.

Furthermore, gunnery training is usually conducted on special ranges, not in rough terrain. The tanks are allowed to approach the target on road surfaces, not cross-country. Shooting is usually from a halt, or from a slow forward approach on a road. The Soviet military press has been highly critical of training routines, suggesting that some units cheat by being informed of the location of targets. The other phase of gunnery training is similarly unrealistic. Target engagement with the co-axial machine gun is designed to simulate engagement against a jeep with a TOW anti-tank missile. The training norm assumes that such a target could be eliminated by three short five- to seven-round machine gun bursts—which is unbelievable.

Because NATO expects to fight outnumbered, considerable stress is placed at engaging targets at maximum range and destroying them in rapid succession. NATO training has been further aided by robust competition, epitomised by the biennial Canadian Army Trophy (CAT) shoot held since 1963. The Canadian Army Trophy competition is something of an Olympics in tank gunnery; it has fostered a considerable degree of competitiveness amongst NATO tankers, with CAT victories a matter of considerable unit and national pride. While CAT results are not necessarily indicative of the average performance expected of NATO tank crews, they do give a clear idea of the goals that they strive to achieve.

The CAT 85 held at the Bergen-Hohne ranges in June 1985 provides a good example, since it mixed older-generation tanks like the Chieftain and M60A3 against current generation tanks like the M1 and Leopard 2. The targets used are 1.90m long by 1.60m high, designed to simulate a partly exposed tank turret front, and are engaged from the halt and on the move ranges varying between 800 and 2,000m. The fastest scoring platoon was an M1 unit with a sizzling average score of a mere 6.2 seconds from target pop-up to destruction. The combined average also found the M1 Abrams to have the quickest engagement time, of 10.2 seconds, while the older Leopard 1s had the slowest average of 16.2 seconds. In terms of accuracy, Dutch Leopard 2s hit 46 out of 48 targets, while the low scorers were a Canadian Leopard C1 team with a very respectable 34 out of 48. The table below provides a quick summary of the results.

Team	Engage-ment Time (seconds)	Hits	Hit Percentage
US M1 Abrams	10.2	44–45	93%
Dutch Leopard 2	11.9	46	96%
German Leopard 2	11.9	42–45	91%
German Leopard 1	16.2	45	93%
Belgian Leopard 1	16.2	41	85%
British Chieftain	13.0	38	79%
US M60A3	14.1	37	77%
Canadian Leopard C1	16.2	34	71%

The results at the Canadian Army Trophy have continued to improve over the years as fire control improvements have been introduced. The most recent CAT shoot, in 1987 at Grafenwohr saw the highest score ever recorded: 22,600 out of a possible 28,000 by an American IPM1 Abrams platoon of

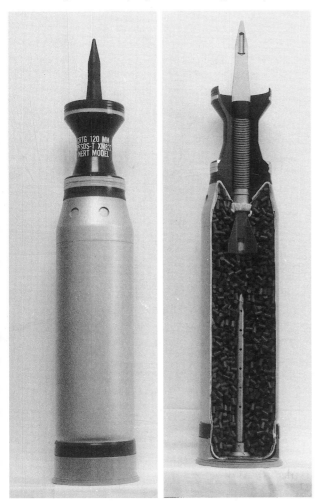

Tank combat in Europe relies on armour-piercing, fin-stabilised, discarding-sabot projectiles (APFSDS) like this American 120mm M827 round. The subcalibre depleted uranium dart projectile is encased in a sabot which falls away as the projectile leaves the barrel. The 120mm ammunition used on German and US tanks has a consumable propellant casing, with only a small metal stub-case remaining after firing. (US Army-APG)

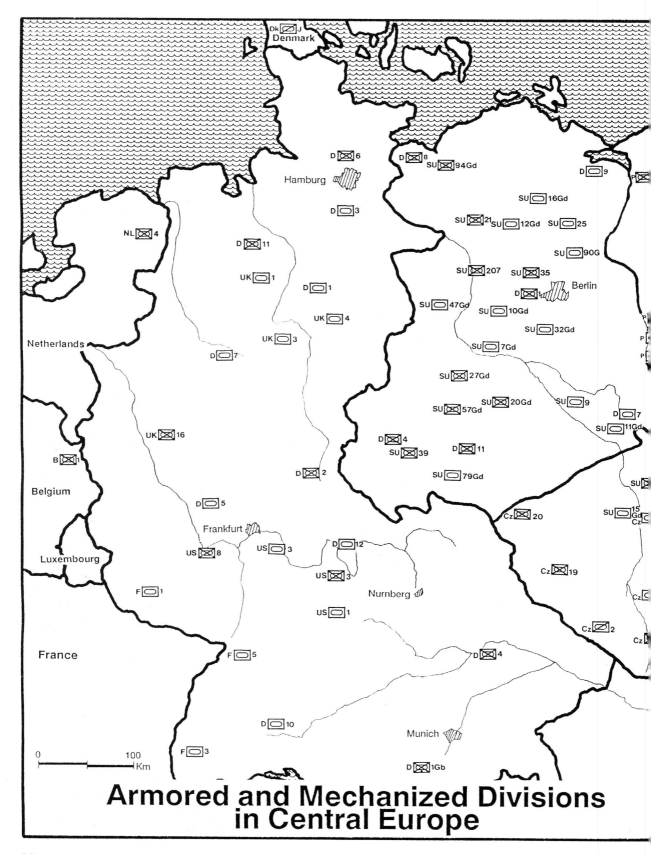

Armored and Mechanized Divisions
in Central Europe

Company D, 4/8th Cavalry. Equally remarkable was the success of several units in engaging targets in spite of indifferent weather conditions like rain and fog.

While the CAT shoots are probably not representative of NATO tank gunnery as a whole, they point to the emphasis placed on rapid target acquisition and engagement in NATO. They also clearly show the capability of the equipment. The Soviet T-72 tank is only capable of firing six rounds per minute due to its autoloader. The US standard is a round every five seconds, or 12 rounds per minute—double the maximum possible on the Soviet tank. US M1 tank training aims at 12 second engagement cycles: it is expected that in 12 seconds, the crew will locate and fire on their opponent at 2,000m, and have a 90 per cent probability of kill. This is considerably faster than the Soviet training norms.

Training also benefits from the quality of training equipment. Tanks are becoming so expensive to operate that a considerable amount of training has to take place on simulators rather than on the tanks themselves. Both the Warsaw Pact and NATO employ simulators, though their design and effectiveness is quite uneven. Computers and digital graphics technology have permitted the development of highly sophisticated simulators which closely mimic real training. One of the finer examples of this type of system is the U-COFT simulator used by the US Army for gunnery training. These are considerably more realistic than 1950s-vintage mechanical trainers which relied on sub-scale target ranges and US Army officers suggest that the improving CAT scores are closely related to the increased amount of realistic training these simulators provide. In general, NATO has a decided edge in the quality of crew training simulators. There has been considerable spin-off from civilian training simulator and aircraft simulator technology in Western Europe and America. The Soviets, although intensely interested in simulators, have not yet begun to field simulators comparable to Western systems, mainly due to

The fighting compartment of the M60A1 tank. This is fairly typical of tanks of its generation: very little electronics evident, and simple optical sights. Here, the tank commander (to the right) uses the optical rangefinder. Compare this with the photo of the M1 interior. (Author)

Another example of 1950s tank technology—the interior of the T-62 tank. This is a view from the commander's seat towards the gunner's station. Soviet tank fire controls tended to be more elementary than American equivalent, even back in the early 1960s when this particular tank was built. (Author)

shortcomings in computer technology.

Tank gunnery and driver training are the building blocks of tank unit training. Individual crew skills are useless unless matched to good troop and platoon leadership, and experience in operating in unit-sized actions. Soviet tank training typically revolves around annual training cycles. Once basic skills are mastered in the beginning half of the training year, the schedule shifts to platoon, company, battalion and regimental exercises. These are usually capped by divisional exercises at the end of the year. Soviet training does not appear to involve extensive force-on-force training, with one unit playing opposing forces. This type of practice is more common in NATO, especially in the US Army. New technology has helped in this respect. Laser simulation devices, like the US Army MILES, the British Simfire, and the German

Talissi systems, add a considerable degree of realism to mock engagements. Tanks are fitted with eye-safe lasers which serve in place of actual gunfire and with laser detection devices. When hit by the laser beam from an opposing tank, the detectors activate an amber beacon signalling that the tank has been killed, and inactivate the opponent's laser device. This makes realistic force-on-force training practical.

The higher expectations of NATO armies compared to the Soviet forces can also be traced to recruitment and crew retention practices. The Soviet Ground Forces rely on conscripts, and there is hardly any NCO retention. It is not simply that Soviet tanker training is rudimentary by NATO standards; what training is acquired is lost when the tankers return to civilian life at the end of their two-year stint. Tank training varies depending on crew position. Certain crew members, usually the driver-mechanic and loader, receive the minimal basic training and are then dispatched to their division or tank training regiments to learn their basic skills. Gunners and tank commanders are frequently given more extensive training, usually a six-month specialist course. A Soviet tank platoon consists of three tanks. Of the crews, only the platoon leader is an officer (lieutenant) and there is a good chance that he is a short-term officer such as a university student fulfilling his mandatory stint of duty. As a result, it is not uncommon to find tank platoons with about a quarter of their troops nearing two years of training, and few if any troops with more than two years of duty. In contrast, NATO tank units invariably include a significant percentage of professional NCOs, serving as tank commanders.

The Soviets seem to appreciate these shortcomings, and reforms may take place over the next few years. During the visit of Marshal S. Akhromeyev to the US tank base at Ft. Hood in 1988, the US Army hosts were surprised at Akhromeyev's lack of interest in the hardware, but his intense curiosity in training and personnel issues. Akhromeyev was apparently surprised to find senior tank sergeants with 17 years of army service and was intrigued to learn that they are paid well enough to support a family. Akhromeyev and his team were equally surprised by the quality of troop barracks and enlisted housing on base. In the Soviet Army NCO pay is too low to adequately support a family, and there is inadequate family support in the form of base housing.

Tank warfare at its elemental level is a war waged by sergeants and enlisted men: tank crews, unlike fighter aircraft crews, are made up primarily of NCOs and enlisted men. NATO tank crew policy varies from country to country, but generally favours the development of professional NCOs to form the backbone of the tank force. The complexity of modern tank designs, as well as the complexity of modern combined-arms tactics, places greater demands on tank commanders than in the past. These skills take years to learn and perfect, and the presence of a cadre of experienced NCO tankers provides a unit with continuity. High gunnery scores, high tank availability rates and rigorous training are very difficult, if not impossible without professional NCOs. And professional NCOs are not possible in an army like the Soviet Ground Forces, where the NCOs have little status

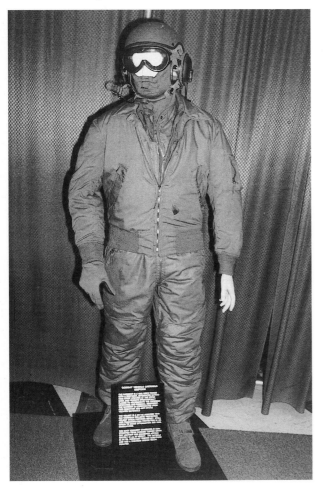

and low pay.

The Balance Sheet

So how do NATO and the Warsaw Pact shape up? At a tactical level, NATO tank units enjoy significant qualitative advantages that would probably translate into disproportionate tank kill ratios when fighting Warsaw Pact vehicles. The Warsaw Pact enjoys sizeable numerical superiority which in many instances could counterbalance NATO's qualitative edge. Tanks alone would not decide the outcome of a conventional war in Europe, but they would play a significant part. The tank issue cannot be wrenched out of the larger context of combined arms combat. Other factors such as logistics, and the performance of other combat arms would directly relate to their performance.

While no grand conclusions about a future war can be drawn from this short book, a few conclusions can be drawn about other issues. This book also makes it clear that conventional arms control will be a very difficult business. It is not as easy to rate the value of the tank as a strategic missile. The value of a tank often depends as much on the infrastructure supporting it, such as crew quality, as it does on technical parameters. Is a German crewed T-72 56 per cent as good as an American M1, and a Soviet-crewed T-72 45 per cent as good as a British Challenger? And how could you tell, short of an actual war?

If anything, these uncertainties act as a deterrant to conventional war in Europe. The Soviets do seem aware of NATO qualitative advantages, and this factor creates nagging doubts about the possibilities of a quick Soviet victory in a conventional contest along the German border.

The Plates

A: NATO Tank Crew Uniforms
NATO tankers uniforms have also been covered in a number of other Osprey publications, notably

The American Combat Vehicle Crewman Uniform displayed on a mannikin. This is the mild weather variant with jacket, Nomex face protector, and experimental rough-finish brown boots. There has been an increased use of Nomex fire-resistant material in NATO crew uniforms to prevent flash burns like those suffered by Israeli tankers in the 1973 war. (Author)

The Czechoslovak Army still depends heavily on the old T-54A and T-54B. The Czechoslovak Army is one of the few Warsaw Pact forces to regularly camouflage-paint its tanks, as seen here.

Elite 16, *NATO Armies Today* (see Plate D2 for a Dutch tanker); American tankers' uniforms are covered in Vanguard 41, *The MI Abrams Tank*, Plate G.

A1: Corporal, 1st Royal Tank Regiment; summer exercise uniform, 1990?

Out-of-the-vehicle dress for warm weather—the respirator/NBC kit satchel is carried at all times under tactical conditions; and the 'Shorty' carbine version of the SA.80 rifle is under consideration as the standard vehicle crew weapon. The black coveralls are the prerogative of the RTR, and all units wear the regiment's black and white tank badge on the upper sleeve; chevrons, in white, are worn on the right only, and a black-on-white name tape on the left breast. Shoulder slide loops identify the unit: red for 1st RTR, yellow for 2nd, blue for 3rd, and green for 4th. The black beret and 'Fear Naught' cap badge are common to all units of RTR.

A1A: British tank commander in NBC clothing

The current 'general issue' NBC suit—favoured for extra warmth in peacetime winter manoeuvres—is shown here. A new Nomex coverall exists, but is not issued in peacetime, as of the time of writing. The current Racal AFV crewman helmet/headset is worn, with the 'respirator/microphone' designed to accompany it—note that the mike boom of the helmet is pushed up out of the way, and a mike lead is attached to the respirator itself. There is one common item missing from this painting: on

manoeuvres in bad weather, it is quite common to see a large umbrella, often in some cheerful commercial livery, rigged upright over the cupola. One feels such comforts would be frowned upon under war conditions.

A2: Bundeswehr tank crewman, summer dress
A3: Bundeswehr tank crewman, winter dress

Bundeswehr tank crews are issued this green coverall, which is worn in all seasons. During summer months it is worn over light clothing, while in winter it is worn over the field jacket with the fur collar pulled out. Plate A2 shows a *Stabsfeldwebel* in the summer pattern, wearing the new tanker's helmet, which vaguely resembles the Soviet cloth helmet, but is better protected. He is wearing a temporary insignia of PzBtl 363, worn during the 1987 Canadian Army Trophy shoot. Insignia on either arm consists of the national tricolour above rank insignia. He is wearing the standard Bundeswehr lace-up boot. Plate A3 shows an *Oberfeldwebel* in the same coverall, but in winter configuration worn over winter field clothing. This tanker is wearing the traditional black beret of the Panzer force, and has on heavier rubber boot covers over the lace-up boots.

B1: Danish Centurion Mk.5/2(Mod), Danish Life Regiment, Jutland Division; NATO Exercise 'Eternal Triangle'

Denmark originally acquired 210 new Centurion Mk 3 tanks in 1954 in 1954 with US funding. Of the remaining Centurions, a total of 106 have been upgraded with the L7A1 105mm gun, Ericsson laser rangefinder sights and AEG Telefunken fire controls. A large fire control and optics package is contained in an armoured container to the right of the main gun tube. The Danish camouflage is reminiscent of British style, although the green is distinctly lighter and more olive. Markings are simple, with a serial number on the turret bin and the regimental crest (inset 1A) on the forward side of the stowage bin.

B2: Norwegian Leopard 1, Stridsvogneskadron, 6th Division, NATO Exercise 'Arrowhead Express' 1988

The Norwegian Army has 78 Leopards, acquired in 1969–71, organised into independent *stridsvognes-kadron* (medium tank squadrons) and three tank battalions. The Leopards are finished in a splinter pattern reminiscent of the Swedish style first adopted on Saab Viggen fighters in the late 1970s. The scheme normally consists of three or four summer colours as seen on Plate B3 below. During the winter a temporary white tempera paint is applied over the lighter summer colours, leaving a three-tone pattern of white, black and NATO dark green. The vehicle carries its tactical markings on the turret side as well as on wooden boxes attached to the rear bustle. The Norwegian Army uses black numerals on an edged yellow rectangle for serial numbers. A pattern of coloured unit insignia, reminiscent of Second World War British practice, identifies the unit; in this case it is '4N' on a yellow and green rectangle, carried on the container on the upper left rear plate of the hull (inset 2A). The serial is often repeated on the front of the vehicle, either on the glacis plate or left fender. The red 'X' is a tape marking used to identify opposing forces during exercises. It is also carried on the front of the searchlight, and sometimes on the hull front.

B3: Norwegian Leopard 1, Stridsvogneskadron, Norwegian Armoured Group

In recent years, some Leopard units have been adopting this complicated summer camouflage scheme. Consisting of patterns of NATO dark green, a lighter olive green, field drab and black.

C1: Soviet T-55A(M), Ukrainian Military District

Over the past few years the Soviet Ground Forces have begun to show an interest in pattern-painted camouflage. Soviet engineer camouflage handbooks have usually included information on camouflage painting, but it seldom saw actual peacetime use. The basic colour, olive drab No. 2 is a very dark black–green, nearly equivalent to US FS 34077. Initially, units began using available stocks of paints ordinarily used for maintenance. These included Black No. 2 (used for vehicle frames, wheel hubs and underframe parts); Bituminous Black No. 4 (steel parts other than underframe, including track shoes); Silver Grey No. 1 (exposed carbon steel parts); Brown No. 2 (carbon steel primer, such as artillery barrels); and Yellow No. 1 (Steel and aluminium primer used in truck cabs, etc.). The Soviets began issuing actual camouflage paints in the mid-1980s, or authorising the use of existing paints for this purpose. The most common colours used in enamel form are ZIL-508M Green; KhV-714 Black; PKhV-6 Sand; PKhV-26 Red-Brown, KhV-113 Dark Brown and KhV-1 White. Soviet manuals show a very conventional pattern which is followed on the example here. Over the base olive drab No. 2 are rolling bands of PKhV-26 Red–Brown and KhV-714 Black. The tactical number is in white. According to Soviet Ground Forces Regulation 50-1982, the numbers are arbitrary, although they may follow a pattern. (For a typical example of the meaning of Soviet tactical

An M1 Abrams during a winter 'Reforger' exercise. The M1 is finished in a temporary winter camouflage scheme using water-based paint. In spite of a great deal of unfounded public criticism, the M1 Abrams has proven to be a very popular tank with US tankers, and has performed well in Europe. (Pierre Touzin)

numbers see Vanguard 37, *Modern Soviet Combat Tanks*, p.34). According to regulations, the number are to be from 20cm to 40cm in height (except on small items) and the width should be $\frac{2}{3}$ the height. In summer months the numbers are white; in winter or desert conditions, red or black.

C2: Czechoslovak T-55A(M)-Kladivo, 1988
The Czechoslovak Army has been using painted camouflage for over 15 years. It is generally based on temporary tempera paints, and is used mainly during summer wargames. The most popular colours are ochre or red-brown as seen here. Although not very noticeable, in this case the red-brown is edged in black. This vehicle is a good example of the heavily retrofitted T-55s now being seen in Warsaw Pact armour units. It has the horseshoe armour on the turret fronts, as well as the locally produced Kladivo fire control system with a laser rangefinder over the main gun, and a wind-sensor at the rear of the turret. The Czechoslovak tricolour is painted on the front of the horseshoe armour, and is repeated (inset 2A).

C3: Soviet T-64B, Central Group of Forces; Czechoslovakia, 1988
Although the Soviet Ground Forces are adopting camouflage on their tanks, this is far from universal; this T-64B is finished in the usual olive drab No. 2. The principal marking is a pattern of white bands, forming a cross when viewed from overhead; the arms of the cross are evident in this view. A white band also extends over the centreline of the vehicle from the centre of the glacis plate, over the turret, and over the engine deck roof (but not the gun barrel). This is one of the more historically common Soviet air identification markings, as used in the invasion of the Baltic states in 1940, the capture of Berlin in 1945, and the invasion of Czechoslovakia in 1968. During peacetime, it is usually used to identify 'opposing forces' during Warsaw Pact exercises. The vehicle markings (inset 3A) are a traditional geometric shape. These shapes deliberately vary. The upper number may be a regimental identifier, and the lower number the individual vehicle. Over the past few years the Soviet Ground Forces have made a more deliberate effort to mark the fuel and stowage panniers on the T-64, T-72 and T-80 tanks. The usual stencilled

markings are ZIP (*zapas, instrumenta i priborov*: spares, tools and accessories) and TOPLIVO (fuel). Enlarged versions of these stencils are shown inset as (3B).

D1: M1A1 Abrams, 64th Armor, US 3rd Infantry Division; Federal Republic of Germany
In the mid-1980s, the Bundeswehr began to push the other NATO countries to adopt a standard NATO tank and combat vehicle scheme. The Germans argued that it was too easy for Warsaw Pact forces to identify the nationality of a vehicle simply by its paint finish. The US, Netherlands and France have begun adopting this scheme already. In the US case, the finish is applied directly at the factory, and this process began in 1987. Not all US tanks in Europe are finished in this fashion, and it is not clear how soon older vehicles will be repainted. The colours used on the US vehicles are FS 30051 Green, FS 34094 Brown and FS 37030 Black.

The US Army has been gradually adopting the practice of fitting unit identification symbols on the turret rear. The inset drawings show the official turret bustle markings laid down in Field Circular No. 71–6 in March 1985. The basic yellow geometric shape discloses the battalion: 1st battalion—28 in. square; 2nd—30 in. high octagon; 3rd—34.5 in. high diamond; 4th—30 in. circle; 5th—30 in. high hexagon. The inner black geometric design identifies the company: A Co.—17 in. square; B Co.—20 in. high octagon; C Co.—23.7 in. high diamond; D Co.—20 in. diameter circle; E Co.—20 in. high hexagon. Platoons are identified by white bars, and individual vehicles are identified by a numeral below the platoon insignia. The inset drawings shown signify: (D1) No. 1 tank, 2nd Plt., C Co., 1st Bn; (D2) No. 3 tank, 3rd Plt., D Co., 3rd Bn.; (D3) No. 4 tank, 1st Plt., A Co., 2nd Bn.; (D4) No. 3 tank, 3rd Plt., B Co., 4th Bn. As will be immediately noticed, this tank from the 3rd Infantry Division uses an entirely different system. (Alternative systems are described in Vanguard 41 *The M1 Abrams Tank*, p. 37 and Vanguard 43, *The M2 Bradley Infantry Fighting Vehicle*, pp.43–44.)

It has become standard practice to paint bumper codes on a sand background. The bumper codes here are '3-I-1-64 HQ-65' and follow the usual US practice. Other markings include the vehicle name on the barrel fume extractor ('Nemesis'); and red

reflective safety tape on one front and rear (one horizontal stripe forward, two horizontal stripes on the rear).

E1:IPM1 Abrams, D Co., 4/8th Cavalry, US 3rd Armored Division, Canadian Army Trophy, 1987

During recent Canadian Army Trophy (CAT) shoots, it has become popular practice to paint cartoon cats on the tanks. This example, from the winning US platoon in 1987, is pretty colourful. On the right side of the turret (1A) is the traditional US armour triangle, with a flash reading 'Canadian Army Trophy'. Superimposed on the drawing is a national eagle and shield design, and a small tank. On the left turret front (1B) is 'Bill the Cat' from the popular *Bloom County* comic strip, seen in his typical frazzled state. Tanks in this unit had the spearhead divisional crest (1C), about 3ft high, attached to the metal plate at the centre of the rear bustle rack in place of the usual tactical insignia. Tanks in the platoon had the platoon names in black or white on the fume extractor, and centred on the upper edge of the bow or gun mantlet. 'Danger Zone' (1D) had the bumper code 'D23', and 'Dry' (seen in the photo here) was 'D65'.

E2:M1 Abrams, US 66th Armor, Canadian Army Trophy-1987

Another contender at CAT 87 was a platoon from 2/66th Armor, which scored fourth. They had some of their tanks finished with this elaborate tiger insignia. The barrel inset (2A) shows the vehicle name, 'Viper', as applied to the fume extractor of one of the tanks.

E3:M1 Abrams, US 3/64 Armor, Canadian Army Trophy 1985

The cat insignia craze started in 1985 with cartoons like this one, showing the lead character of the 'Garfield' cartoon strip, riding an APFSDS round. The bumper code on this vehicle was '3-I-3-64 △A-12'.

F1:Leopard 2, 3/PzBtl 124, 4.Panzergrenadier Division, 1986

The Bundeswehr pioneered the new NATO three-tone paint scheme, and it first entered widespread use on new-production Leopard 2 tanks. The German terms for the scheme call for *Bronzegrun*, *Teerschwarz* and *Lederbraun*. German tank insignia have gradually become more colourful over the past decade, using a combination of simplified tactical insignia derived from Second World War Panzer insignia, and the occasional use of heraldic unit insignia. In this case the divisional insignia, a yellow Y over an oval in a shield, is stencilled on the turret front (inset 1A). The battalion insignia, a white jester on a bright green shield with white border, is painted towards the rear of the turret side. Behind the battalion insignia is a red 'B' on a black square; this marking is on a removable plate. The red 'X' is a manoeuvre marking, usually signifying opposing forces. Small tactical insignia, which used to be painted in white, are now painted in a pale blue drab. These include the weight/bridging numbers on the right fender ('60 7') and the unit tactical insignia ('3-124' on either side of tank unit map symbol). The licence plate, in this case 'Y41-1763', is carried on a thin white rectangle with black trim on the upper lip of the hull plate.

F2: *Leopard 2, 2/PzBtl 363, 12 Panzer Division, NATO Exercise 'Certain Sentinel'*

A typical example of current Bundeswehr markings. The large orange rectangle and unit code are typical NATO exercise markings, and are also carried on the upper hull front, which will be noticed by careful examination of the front view of the vehicle seen in F2A. The tactical insignia at the turret rear is a German equivalent of the US pattern. Some additional examples are shown below the side profile, but details are lacking. It would appear that the shape indicates company, and the vertical bars indicate platoon (with the fourth platoon having the upper portion of the company insignia filled in as shown in the insignia at the far left and far right). In terms of unit insignia, the tank carries the red bison (derived from the old wartime PzRgt7 insignia) on the armoured door of the night sight on the right turret front. This is shown in more detail in inset drawing (2B); typical unit tactical insignia are shown at 2C.

F3: *Leopard 2, 2/PzBtl 244, 1 Gebirgs Division*

This rear view of a Leopard from PzBtl 244 shows some of the local variation permitted in unit

A Leopard 2 of the 43rd Tank Battalion of the Dutch Army with 1st Netherlands Corp in Germany. The Dutch Army was the first NATO army after Germany to field the Leopard 2. (Pierre Touzin)

insignia. This particular tank did not have the traditional three-digit number on the turret side. Instead, four medium blue strips are painted on the container on the left rear turret. On the right turret rear is the company insignia, painted on a removeable plate. This insignia is shown in more detail in the inset drawing (3A). Many tank units have these company and battalion heraldic designs, but they are usually attached only for parades, displays or other special occasions.

G1: *East German T-72G, 9.Panzerdivision, DDR, 1987*

The East German NVA does not usually camouflage-paint its tanks except during winter exercises, when white tempera is applied. There are no official patterns, and the appearance varies considerably depending upon the crew. Shown inset are the tank insignia for East Germany, Poland, Bulgaria and Hungary.

H1: *Dutch Leopard 2A1, 43e Tankbataljon, 41e Panzerbrigade, 1 Korps; Canadian Army Trophy 1985*

The Dutch Leopard 2A1s are finished in overall German *bronzegrun* as on delivery. The tanks from the 43rd Tank Battalion were very colourfully marked during the CAT 85 competition, with the Dutch national colours painted across the engine exhaust. The CAT 85 logo was cleverly designed to give the lead 'C' a lion-like shape. In front of the CAT85 slogan are a couple of circular 'zaps'; it has become common practice at these international meets to place various types of decals and stickers ('zaps') on the tanks of opposing teams. More typical of the normal service markings are the vehicle name in black ('Agoeti', 'Attila', etc.); the battalion crest on the turret front in yellow (1A); and the usual style of NATO map-symbol unit insignia. On the front and rear fenders, the Dutch flag is carried to the right and the 1 Korps emblem to the left. The insignia shown here (1B) is a considerably simplified version of the 1 Korps badge, probably due to the small size in which it is painted. The serial number is painted in black on a yellow rectangle.

H2: *Greek Leopard 1A3, 1986*

The Greek Army ordered 106 Leopard 1A3s in 1981 as a part of a general modernisation programme. The Greek Army has begun painting

its vehicles in a scheme very reminiscent of the 1970s US Army MERDC pattern, with a four-tone scheme of field drab, dark green, black and sand. The blue and white national insignia is carried on the turret side; it is shown inset.

H3: Canadian Leopard C1, Royal Canadian Dragoons; Canadian Army Trophy, 1987

Like some of the other units participating at CAT-87, the Canadian entries had a suitable cat cartoon, in this case, the ever-suave Pink Panther (3B). The Canadian Leopards are rather plainly marked, with the national maple leaf insignia (3A) in black with white outline. A 'zap' can be seen over the Pink Panther, and another (a US flag) on the fume extractor on the gun barrel. The national flag and a unit pennant are flown from the aerials.

I: T-62E, Berlin Separate Tank Regt, Soviet 6th Guards Motor Rifle Division; Turkestan Military District, 1986

This T-62E with horseshoe armour is fairly typical of the new trend towards camouflage painting on Soviet tanks. The scheme consists of olive drab No.

Although Austria is not a NATO country, there is a high probability that it would be dragged into any conventional war in Central Europe. The mainstay of its tank force is the M60 tank, with 120 M60A1 and 50 M60A3 tanks in service. One of the few changes on the Austrian vehicles is the provision of an AEG-Telefunken XSW-30-U infrared searchlight instead of the American model. (HBF-Austrian Army)

2 with a sprayed squiggle pattern of black. This unit was stationed in Afghanistan, being withdrawn to the Turkestan Military District in 1986. The scheme has been seen in other parts of the USSR, but seems to be favoured in the Central Asian military districts. The only markings on the tank are a simple diamond in a circular tactical marking, carried on the front of the horseshoe armour; and a Guards insignia on the searchlight cover. The four circular inset drawings show (left to right) the T-62E's unit emblem, and the insignia of 225th, 233rd and 235th Tank Regiments. These latter insignia are interesting in that they show the traditional divisional pattern of Soviet tank markings, with a slight variation for each of the tank division's regiments. The large inset drawing is the insignia of the Soviet Group of Forces Germany (GSFG). This is usually limited to tactical vehicles, and is rarely carried on armoured vehicles.

A T-80 tank with the full array of explosive reactive armour. The T-80s fitted with reactive armour have a reconfigured skirt which may contain additional ballistic protection in the forward half. This particular vehicle carries a regimental or divisional symbol in white on the rear stowage box.

J1, 1A: *Chieftain, Armoured Squadron, Berlin Infantry Brigade, BAOR*

The armoured vehicles of this squadron are undoubtedly the most strikingly painted armoured vehicles in Europe. In the mid-1980s, the former commander of the Berlin Brigade's armoured squadron, Lt.Col. Clendon Daukes (later commander of the 4th/7th Royal Dragoon Guards), developed this unique urban camouflage scheme. Daukes suggested that the conventional green and black scheme was hardly appropriate in an urban environment, hence this imaginative pattern in white, grey and brown.

J2, 2A: *Challenger, The Royal Hussars, 1 Armoured Division, BAOR*

British tanks with BAOR are finished in 'Light Olive Green' and black camouflage, though some have 'Dark Olive'. In keeping with the trends towards low visibility markings, the vehicle tac number ('41') within the unit sign (a square) is in

black on green (2B). However, the marking facing rearward (2C) is on a removable cloth panel, and painted in white for better visibility for friendly forces. Markings at the rear include the regimental crest (2D), the serial number, vertical white bar station-keeping marking and a Union flag.

K: *T-80, Group of Soviet Forces-Germany; DDR, 1988*

This T-80 with reactive armour is in overall olive drab No. 2. In recent years, Soviet tanks have been sporting *bort* numbers over most of the small, removable fittings. These (from the Russian *bort* 'side') are the usual three-digit tactical number specified in Soviet Ground Forces regulation. The Field Regulation 50-1982 permitted *bort* numbers to be added to any turret equipment that was removable. This is believed to stem from the usual army problem of one crew stealing bits from another tank when inspection time approaches. It is a special problem on the T-80 due to the placement of the engine hatches, and the proliferation of equipment on the rear of the turret: to gain access to parts of the engine, it is necessary to remove a good deal of the kit packed above the hatch on the turret rear. As a result, many crews leave off much of this equipment, making it more vulnerable to loss or theft.

As a result of the reactive armour, the normal large *bort* number is not possible. In some T-80 units, the insignia is moved down to the side panniers. As is traditional in Guards units, the Guards insignia is painted on the front of the turret searchlight.

Inset (A) is the insignia of tank units participating in the 1981 Zapad/81 war games. Inset (B) is that of an unidentified tank regiment in the Byelorussian military district. Insets (C) and (D) are insignia of two unidentified tank regiments from the Central Group of Forces in Czechoslovakia.

L: Warsaw Pact Tank Uniforms

Warsaw Pact crew uniforms are remarkably similar, relying for the most part on black coveralls, topped with the ubiquitous black Soviet tanker's helmet. Details of Soviet tanker's uniforms can be found in Elite 12, *Inside the Soviet Army Today*, Plate F; and Polish tanker's garb in Elite 10, *Warsaw Pact Ground Forces*.

L1: Czechoslovak tank crewman

As throughout most of the Warsaw Pact, Czechoslovak tankers normally wear a simple black coverall over their normal field fatigues. The basic coverall is shown in Elite 10, *Warsaw Pact Ground Forces*, Plate C4. The *cetar* (corporal) illustrated wears the black canvas tanker's jacket and coveralls over the normal battle dress. Rank insignia is carried (as three pips) on a small cloth rectangle over the right breast.

L2: East German tank lieutenant

Although the East German NVA does have the usual sort of black coverall for its tank troops (see Elite 10, *Warsaw Pact Ground Forces*, Plate B2), the tankers more usually wear the normal stone-brown *kampfanzug* (field dress) common to the entire army. The only distinctive element is the ubiquitous cloth tanker's helmet. Rank insignia are carried on the shoulder boards—in this case, two pips, designating a lieutenant.

L3: Soviet Ground Forces Observer, NATO Exercises, 1988

This figure is indicative of the changing relations between NATO and the Warsaw Pact. One of the 'confidence-building measures' introduced to reduce tension between NATO and the Warsaw Pact has been the decision to permit observers from both sides to attend large alliance wargames. The Soviet contingent at recent exercises has been wearing this new-pattern battledress. The basic cut of the uniform is similar to that adopted in Afghanistan in the mid-1980s, including the new peaked cap. However, the camouflage pattern had previously been confined to a special uniform issued to flight crews and élite airmobile units, of a somewhat different cut. The shoulder insignia is also unusual in that it is embroidered, not the usual cheap plastic-on-felt. The lace-up boots are probably private purchase or special issue. No rank insignia were carried on this uniform, although subdued rank insignia may be used in line units.

Notes sur les planches en couleur

A Vous trouverez également des uniformes d'équipages de chars dans d'autres ouvrages Osprey, *Elite 16 NATO Armies Today* et *Vanguard 41 The M1 Abrams Tank*.

A1 Tenue caractéristique de manoeuvres; la combinaison noire, le ceinturon et le béret et l'écusson sur la manche droite, sont spécifiques aux RTR, les boucles de couleur sur l'épaule identifiant chacun des quatre régiments. Il porte un kit NBC et la version carabine du fusil SA.80 **A1A** Combinaison protectrice NBC et casque d'équipage britannique actuel. **A2** Combinaison portée sur la tenue légère d'été; nouveau casque pour char de la Bundeswehr; insigne temporaire de PzBtl 363, porté pour l'épreuve de tir CAT; insigne de grade et écusson national sur chaque bras. **A3** Même combinaison portée sur la veste à col de fourrure pour l'hiver; béret noir des troupes de char; couvre-bottes de caoutchouc pour l'hiver.

B1 Equipement de contrôle de tir modernisé dans le conteneur blindé à droite du canon. Écusson régimentaire (**B1A**) à l'avant du coffre de magasinage. **B2** Même peinture de camouflage de style suédois que **B3**, mais recouvert d'une couche de peinture blanche en hiver. Même insigne que **B2A** sur le côté supérieur gauche à l'arrière de la caisse. Le 'X' rouge est un marquage de maneouvre temporaire. **B3** Camouflage d'été récemment adopté.

C1 Les chars soviétiques sont apparus récemment avec des finitions de camouflage à base de vert olive, associé à du noir, du sable, du brun-rouge, du brun foncé ou du blanc. C'est le modèle présenté dans le manuel. **C2** L'on voit

Farbtafeln

A NATO-Uniformen der Panzerbesatzungen werden ausserdem in anderen Büchern von Osprey behandelt, und zwar in Elite 16 *NATO Armies Today* und Vanguard 41 *The M1 Abrams Tank*.

A1 Die typische Manöveruniform setzt sich aus einem schwarzen Anzug, Gürtel, Gelduniformmütze, dem rechten Ärmelabzeichen—welches von der RTR getragen wird—und farbigen Schulterschlaufen, die von den vier Regimentern verwendet werden, zusammen. Darüber hinaus gehört die NBC-Ausrüstung und die Karabinerversion des SA.80 Gewehrs dazu. **A1A** NBC-Schutzanzug und derzeitiger britischer Besatzungshelm. **A2** Ein Overall, der über der leichten Sommeruniform getragen wird; neue Panzerhelme der Bundeswehr; vorübergehende Insignien der PzBtl 363 beim CAT Schützenwettbewerb. **A3** Es handelt sich um den gleichen Overall, der über dem mit Pelz besetzten Kragen der Winterjacke getragen wird. Schwarze Felduniformmütze der Panzersoldaten sowie aus Gummi hergestellte Stiefelschützer.

B1 Verbesserte Feuerbekämpfungsgeräte in gepanzerten Behältern, rechts vom Schnellfeuergeschütz. Das Regimentswappen (**B1A**) ist vorn auf dem Verstaukanister zu erkenne. **B2** Das gleiche, im schwedischen Stil gehaltene Tarnmuster wie B3, welches jedoch für den Winter mit Weiss überstrichen wurde. Die Insignien sind wie in B2A und befinden sich am linken, oberen Ende des Panzers. Das rote 'X' ist eine vorübergehende Manövermarkierung. **B3** Dieses Sommertarnmuster wurde vor kurzem eingeführt.

depuis longtemps de l'ochre ou du brun-rouge peint sur une base verte au cours des manœuvres d'été en Tcécoslovaquie; ici le brun-rouge est légèrement bordé de noir. Notez le blindage de la tourelle amélioré, en 'fer-à-cheval'. **C3** Cette peinture de camouflage est loin d'être universelle. Le marquage familier de reconnaissance aérienne à croix blanche marque ici les 'forces ennemies' pendant les manœuvres. Le marquage **C3A** indique probablement le régiment, au-dessus du numéro de char. **C3B** présente des marquages au tampon sur les outils (en haut) et le magasin à combustible remarqués sur de nombreux chars soviétiques.

D Nouveau modèle de l'OTAN en vert, brun et noir. Les marquages à l'arrière de la tourelle ont des formes identifiant les bataillons—du 1er au 5ème, elles sont respectivement carrées, octogonales, en diamant, circulaires et hexagonales. La forme noire intérieure identifie les Compagnies de A à E—carrée, octogonale, en diamant, circulaire et hexagonale. Les traits blancs verticaux identifient les pelotons, au-dessus des numéros individuels de chars. Pour les autres systèmes, veuillez vous reporter à *Vanguard 41*, *The M1 Abrams Tank* et *43, The M2 Bradley*. Les noms des chars apparaissent sur les canons.

E1 Les marquages spéciaux de tourelle (**E1A**, **1B**) indiquent qu'il s'agit de la compétition annuelle, pour laquelle les dessins de 'chat' sont populaires; l'insigne de la division dans la forme (**E1C**) est exposé sur une plaque à l'arrière de la tourelle. D'autres détails de dessins montrent d'autres combinaisons de marquages.

F1 Insigne de division (**E1A**) avec 'croix rouge' de manœuvre sur l'avant de la tourelle, 'bouffon' blanc sur le bouclier vert, sur le flanc arrière de la tourelle; le code de pont '60 7' et l'insigne d'unité tactique sont peints en bleu ciel sur les pare-chocs. **F2, 2A** Le grand marquage orange est pour les manœuvres; l'écusson du bataillon **F2B** rappelle celui de l'ancien Panzer-Regiment 7; insigne tactique—trois exemples sont présentés en détail au-dessous de la vue latérale du char—ils indiquent la compagnie et le peloton, mais le système exact est inconnu. **F3** Notez les raies bleues; ce char ne portait pas le numéro courant à trois chiffres sur les flancs de la tourelle; l'écusson héraldique de la compagnie (**F3A**) se trouve sur une plaque amovible, pour les parades, etc.

G1 Il n'y a pas de réglementation de modèle officiel de camouflage et chaque équipage applique probablement selon des dessins différents la couche de peinture blanche pour l'hiver. Des vues détaillées montrent les marquages nationaux de la République démocratique d'Allemange, de la Pologne, de la Hongrie et de la Bulgarie.

H1 Marquages de couleur caractéristiques pour les épreuves CAT, y compris le nom de char 'Agoeti', insigne de bataillon (**H1a**) et de Corps (**H1b**). **H2** Le camouflage grec ressemble au modèle US MERDC, avec écusson national seulement. **H3** Ecusson national de feuille d'érable; dessin de la 'Panthère rose' pour l'épreuve CAT; le drapeau US sur le canon et l'insigne au-dessus de la panthère sont des 'zaps'—des auto-collants fixés par des équipages en visite d'autres équipes.

I Notez le blindage de la tourelle en 'fer à cheval', et le camouflage noir-sur-olive. Des vues détaillées montrent l'insigne du Groupe des Forces soviétiques-Allemagne; et (de gauche à droite) le marquage de l'unité sur la tourelle de ce char, avec ceux des autres régiments indiqués.

J1, 1A Camouflage urbain, spécial, conçu par le commandant de l'escadron de chars berlinois. **J2, 2A** Ancien style de camouflage britannique et marquages d'unité tactique (**J2B, C**) et petit écusson régimentaire (**J2D**) sur l'arrière gauche de la caisse.

K Blindage réactif empêchant de marquer en gros les numéros de 'bort' sur la tourelle, ils sont marqués maintenant en petit sur les boites de tourelle et/ou le côté des plaques de suspension. Toutes les pièces amovibles doivent porter leur numéro de 'bort' (voir vue arrière)—les équipages se volent souvent les uns les autres lorsqu'il y a risque imminent de revue. Des vues détaillées présentent l'insigne des Gardes, qui se porte normalement sur les couvercles de projecteurs des unités pertinentes, et l'insigne des jeux de guerre (A) Zapad/81; une unité non identifiée en Biélorussie (B); deux unités non identifiées en Tchécoslovaquie (C, D).

L1 Insigne de grade à trois points porté à droite sur la poitrine. **L2** Bien que l'on porte la combinaison noire du Pacte de Varsovie, l'uniforme de camouflage de toute cette armée est plus courant pour le combat; le grade est indiqué sur les pattes d'épaule. **L3** Nouvel uniforme de camouflage d'observateurs, remarqué lors d'exercises de l'OTAN, de même couple que l'uniforme de combat ordinaire introduit en Afghanistan vers le milieu des années 1980.

C1 In jüngster Zeit wurden sowjetische Panzer mit einem Tarnmuster versehen. Als Grundfarbe wird Olivgrün in Verbindung mit Schwarz, Sandfarben, Rotbraun, Dunkelbraun oder Weiss verwendet. Dieses Farbschema ist im Handbuch abgebildet. **C2** Im Laufe der tschechoslowakischen Sommermanöver sind Ocker und Rotbraun seit längerem durch die Grundfarbe Grün ersetzt worden. In dieser Abbildung wurden die rotbraunen Farbbereiche mit einer dünnen, schwarzen Linie umrandet. Zu beachten ist der weiterentwickelte hufeisenförmige Panzerturm. **C3** Tarnbemalung ist nicht überall üblich. Das bekannte weisse Kreuz, zur Erkennung durch Lufteinheiten, kennzeichnet im Laufe dieser Manöver 'feindliche Truppen'. Die Markierung **C3A** bezieht sich wahrscheinlich auf das Regiment über der Panzernummer. **C3B** Die mit Schablone aufgezeichneten Geräte (oben) und der Tankbehälter, sind auf vielen sowjetischen Panzern zu sehen.

D Das neue Farbschema der NATO: Grün, Braun und Schwarz. Die rückwärtigen Panzerturmmarkierungen haben gelbe Abzeichen, die das Bataillon identifizieren, d. h. 1. bis 5. Bataillon haben dementsprechend ein quadratisches, achteckiges, rautenförmiges, rundes und sechseckiges Abzeichen. Das innere schwarze Abzeichen weist auf die Kompanie von A bis E hin und ist quadratisch, achteckig, rautenförmig, rund oder sechseckig. Zwei weisse vertikale Streifen werden vom Zug getragen, und zwar über den unterschiedlichen Panzernummern. Andere Insignien sind aus Vanguard 41, *The M1 Abrams Tank* sowie 43, *The M2 Bradley* zu entnehmen. Die Panzernamen erscheinen auf dem Geschützrohr.

E1 Spezielle Panzerturmmarkierungen (**E1A**, **1B**) deuten auf den alljährliche Wettbewerb hin, für die die 'Katzen'-Cartoons bekannt sind. Die Divisionsinsignie in der Form (**E1C**) ist auf einer Platte am rückwärtigen Teil des Turmes angebracht. Andere detaillierte Zeichnungen führen eine abwechslende Kombination von Markierungen.

F1 Die Divisionsinsignie (**F1A**) mit dem 'roten Kreuz' ist im Manöver vorn auf dem Panzerturm zu sehen. Die Bataillonsinsignie setzt sich aus einem weissen 'Hofnarr' auf einem grünen Schild zusammen, das hinten am Panzerturm befestigt ist. Der Brückenkode '60 7' und die taktische Einheitsinsignie sind in balssblau gehalten und sind an den Schutzblechen angebracht. **F2, 2A** Die grosse orangefarbene Markierung ist für Manöver bestimmt. Das Bataillonswappen **F2B** erinnert an das alte Panzer-Regiment 7. Die taktischen Insignien—drei Beispiele werden unten auf der Panzerseite gezeigt—lassen die Kompanie und den Zug erkennen, das genaue System ist jedoch unbekannt. **F3** Bemerkenswert sind die blauen Streifen. Diesem Panzer fehlen die übliche dreistellige Nummer auf der Seite des Gewehrrohres. Das heraldische Kompanieabzeichen (**F3A**) ist auf einer Platte angebracht, die bei Paraden abgenommen werden kann.

G Es existiert kein offizielles Tarnmuster, und es ist anzunehmen, dass jede Besatzung die weisse Winterübermalung in unterschiedlichen Mustern anbringt. Detailaufnahmen zeigen die nationalen Markierungen der Deutschen Demokratischen Rebulik, von Polen, Ungarn und Bulgarien.

H1 Die typischen farbenfrohen Markierungen für den 'Cat'-Wettbewerb beinhalten den Panzernamen 'Agoeti', das Bataillon (**H1A**) und die Korpsinsignie (**H1B**). **H2** Das griechische Tarnmuster erinnert an das US MERDC, welches nur die nationale Insignie birgt. **H3** Die nationale Ahornblattinsignie. Die 'rosarote Panther'-Cartoon für den CAT Wettbewerb. Die amerikanische Flagge, die Insignie über den Panther werden 'zaps' gennant, und werden von besuchenden Besatzungen oder anderen Teams angebracht.

I Auffallend ist der 'hufeisenförmige' Panzerturm und die mit Schwarz versehene olivgrüne Tarnbemalung. Detailaufnahmen zeigen die Insignien der Gruppe Sowjetischer Truppen in Deutschland. (Von links nach rechts) die Einheitsmarkierung dieses Panzerturms, der mit den anderen Regimentersmarkierungen versehen ist.

J1, 1A Ein spezieller Stadttarnanstrich, der von einem Berliner Panzergeschwader entwickelt wurde. **J2, 2A** Im alten Stil gehaltene britische Tarnbemalung und taktische Einheitsmarkierungen (**J2B, C**), sowie das kleine Regimentswappen (**J2D**), links hinten am Rumpf.

K Reaktivwirkende Panzerung lässt keine grossen Panzerturm-'Bort'-Nummern zu, die nunmehr kleiner sind und auf dem Turmkasten und/oder an der Seite der Aufhängungsbleche zu sehen sind. Sämtliche abnehmbaren Teile sollten mit dieser Nummer versehen sein (siehe Rückansicht), da Besatzungen oftmals voneinander stehlen, wenn Inspektionen bevorstehen. Detailaufnahmen zeigen die Wacheninsignien, welche sich gewöhnlich auf der Hülle des Suchscheinwerfers, der entsprechenden Einheiten und den Insignien der Zapad/81 Kriegsspiele (A) befinden. Eine nicht identifizierte Einheit in Weissrussland (B). Zwei nicht identifizierte Einheiten in der Tschechoslowakei (C, D).

L1 Ranginsignien, aus drei Punkten bestehend, wurden auf der linken Brusthälfte getragen. **L2** Obgleich es sonst in Warschauer Paktstaaten üblich ist die schwarzen Overalls zu tragen, trifft man den Kampftarnanzug häufiger an, der von dieser Armee getragen wird. Die Rangabzeichen befinden sich an den Schulterstreifen. **L3** Eine neue Tarnuniform, die von Beobachtern bei den NATO-Übungen getragen wurde, ist wie die schlichte Kampuniform geschnitten und wurde Mitte der achtziger Jahre in Afghanistan eingeführt.